This Christmas unwrap the gift of *Finding* [...] Christmas story with fresh wit, insight, prac[...] attention to a facet of how the transcendent [...] than any of us can ever descend to come to us in person, in Jesus. I loved the prayers at the end of each reading—prayers reminding us that Jesus prays for us.

—ADELE AHLBERG CALHOUN, co-senior pastor Redeemer Community Church, Needham, MA; author of *The Spiritual Disciplines Handbook*, *Invitations from God*, and *True You*

Every year I use an Advent devotional for the days preceding Christmas, and this year it will most definitely be my friend Jane Rubietta's *Finding the Messiah*. Each day's selection is a well-woven story featuring the unpredictable cast of characters and events chosen by God to play a role in the coming of the Christ child. Though familiar, these vignettes are fresh and vibrant in the retelling, with definite parallels to my own twenty-first-century life. My favorite part might just be the daily benediction—words of God praying over me. Thank you, Jane, for keeping the meaningful and magnificent in our Advent journey.

—LUCINDA SECREST MCDOWELL, author of *Live These Words*, EncouragingWords.net

Jane Rubietta's *Finding the Messiah* is so beautifully written that it captivates me, drawing me in to experience the story of the birth of Christ in a new and fresh way. Rubietta has an unusual way of expressing new ironies in the age-old original Christmas story. I love that! Through these Advent devotionals, you'll be reading the familiar story again, but seeing it as if for the first time. You're going to love this book.

—DIANNE E. BUTTS, author *Prophecies Fulfilled in the Birth of Jesus* and *Deliver Me*

Jane Rubietta brings a sensitivity to her writing that establishes an immediate bond between Jane and her readers. Her insights are wise, her lessons are practical, and her message is encouraging. Read and be refreshed!

—DENNIS E. HENSLEY, author of over fifty books, including *Jesus in the 9 to 5*; director of professional writing program, Taylor University

Finding the Messiah is a lovely journey to the miraculous life found in Bethlehem. This is a devotional that is also a study in discipleship. It carries readers to the manger, telling the story of Mary and Joseph in a beautiful, exquisite manner. More than a deeply personal Bible study in devotion, this is also a perfect discipleship tool for small groups.

—KATHI MACIAS, award-winning author of more than forty books, including *The Singing Quilt*

In *Finding the Messiah*, Jane Rubietta leads us on a captivating journey to Bethlehem. Her writing is powerful, visual, and impactful. Jane is a gifted wordsmith who captures the essence of developing an intimate connection with God while challenging the reader to do the same. This book is filled with practical applications and opportunities for personal reflection on the birth of our savior. Don't miss it!

—CAROL KENT, speaker, best-selling author of *When I Lay My Isaac Down* and *Unquenchable*

These are transformational devotionals with great depth. Jane offers a fresh and compelling vision of the journey to Bethlehem. But more than rich words, she has coupled biblical truth with practical ways in which to personally walk from darkness to dawn. There is rich and practical depth in these pages.

—JO ANNE LYON, General Superintendent, The Wesleyan Church

Jane Rubietta invites us on a journey from darkness to dawn that will surprise and inspire you. Packed with Scripture and written with personal witness and wisdom, this twenty-eight-day adventure calls us to not only understand, but also live in the promise of full, new life.

—ANDREA SUMMERS, director of ministry for women, The Wesleyan Church

With real-life stories and engaging insight from the Bible, Jane leads readers from darkness to dawn to make our Lord's birth real in our lives. What a brilliant connection! Let Jane lead you there—where the story of our Savior comes alive and the season of Advent resounds with joy.

—THADDEUS BARNUM, author of *Real Identity* and *Real Love*, senior pastor of Church of the Apostles, Fairfield, CT

Jane Rubietta takes us on a reflective spiritual journey during Advent with powerful insights along the way. *Finding the Messiah* brings beautiful stillness to the soul for those overwhelmed by holiday chaos. This book is more than a casual read. It is a heartfelt experience.

—MARK O. WILSON, author of *Purple Fish* and *Filled Up, Poured Out*, senior pastor, Hayward Wesleyan Church, Hayward, WI

FINDING
THE MESSIAH

FROM DARKNESS TO DAWN— THE BIRTH OF OUR SAVIOR

Jane Rubietta

Jane Rubietta

JS. 9:2

wphonline.com

Copyright © 2014 by Jane Rubietta
Published by Wesleyan Publishing House
Indianapolis, Indiana 46250
Printed in the United States of America
ISBN: 978-0-89827-902-3
ISBN (e-book): 978-0-89827-903-0

Library of Congress Cataloging-in-Publication Data

Rubietta, Jane.
  Finding the Messiah : from darkness to dawn--the birth of our Savior / Jane
Rubietta.
      pages cm
   ISBN 978-0-89827-902-3 (pbk.)
1. Advent--Prayers and devotions. I. Title.
   BV40.R83 2014
   242'.332--dc23
                              2014016664

Dedicated with hope
For all of us who seek light
In the darkness of our world
And with gratitude
To the One who invites us on the greatest adventure
Ever

CONTENTS

Acknowledgements	9
Introduction	10
An Advent Confession	12
Week 1 of Advent	17
Week 2 of Advent	47
Week 3 of Advent	81
Week 4 of Advent	113
A Closing Word	150
About the Author	156

A free group leader's guide is available for download at
www.wphresources.com/findingthemessiah.

ACKNOWLEDGEMENTS

Thank you is inadequate, but . . . thank you.

To the creatives in my life who daily hold my heart to the flame. To name a few: Lin Johnson, Lynn Austin, Cleo Lampos, Ellen Binder, Tish Suk. You have prayed for me, loved me, called me on the carpet, and called me to accountability.

To the excellent team at Wesleyan Publishing House—you all have invited me deeper into the Scriptures, deeper into faith, and deeper into excellence.

To my children, who give me a reason every single day to live toward the light.

To my husband, who loves me in spite of me, encouraging me and fanning the flame the gifts God gives me.

To my Savior, the Messiah, who called me and ever calls me out of the darkness and into his glorious light.

INTRODUCTION

The promise came to a world shrouded in darkness, a land where heaven's light dimmed far too soon after creation's first dawn. Prophets and priests, scholars and sheepherders, day laborers and the poorest of the poor sighed and looked up, searching for the One to come, the One who would again split the darkness with light. The One who would retrieve what was lost in Eden. The One who would shatter their chains of oppression and sin, of sadness and blindness.

The world waited, groaning in the long dark night of its soul, longing for relief. Waiting, perhaps without knowing for what it groaned. And then, waiting some more in the thick, silent blackness devoid of God's voice and deaf to God's presence.

And to this season, we come, too. We enter the twenty-eight days of Advent with a year's worth, or perhaps a lifetime's worth, of groaning behind us, the accumulation of debt and doubt, of dread and discouragement. The chains of our past and present clank about our ankles. Some days we don't know how much longer we can press forward, because the gas in our tank of determination hovers near empty. The thought of gutting out another year exhausts us. Our souls sigh; our hearts yearn; our relationships strain under the toil of waiting, watching, and wondering whether we will make it through. And we ask, "Is this finally the year that the Promised One comes, the year he scatters the shadows and shatters our fears and wraps us in the warm light that is night-rending love and forgiveness?"

We come to Advent, wondering if this will be the year when we notice. Notice the light, notice Emmanuel, *God with us*. Notice that Christ's advent actually makes a difference in a world dark with fear and oppression, makes a difference in our lives, personally.

If you have arrived at Advent, at the coming, with doubts, dragging chains of disbelief, disenchantment, and discouragement, welcome. You are not alone. And if you enter this season with a harried heart and a furrowed brow, welcome. You are not alone. If your moanings feel louder than the quiet, subtle hope tucked behind the noise of the world's Christmas season, then welcome. You are not alone.

And that is the good news, isn't it? That in this darkness, in this aching nighttime, we are not alone. Christ comes. This year, just as more than two millennia ago, Christ comes. Christ pierces the darkness with his light. Christ says, "I am the Light of the World." And the darkness, still, cannot extinguish that Light.

This Advent, we face the shadows, and embrace the Light. And we learn that "even the darkness will not be dark to you; the night will shine like the day, for darkness is as light to you" (Ps. 139:12). This year, may Advent pierce the deep darkness of this world and of our lives.

AN ADVENT CONFESSION

I'm a little red-faced and anxious that underneath all my thoughts of Advent, I feel guilty. This is not a ho-ho-ho book. No fa-la-la anywhere. No "Here's how to have a merry Christmas" hints, fail-safe, time-tested, and photo-shoot ready. No clever jingles to jangle around in our soul's pockets. But before traveling too far down that path to moroseness, I remember: the holidays have turned into a trumped-up excuse to spend money, gain weight, help retailers, try to make up for what we haven't given people all year or maybe all their lives long. The holidays have become a great attempt at atonement for our deficits with others and maybe our deficits with our souls.

To find the Messiah, we likely need not look under the Christmas tree.

Recently, I jotted a list from memory of the Advent characters: Herod, Zechariah, Gabriel, Elizabeth, Mary, John, wise men, shepherds, angels, Simeon, and Anna. And only after mulling over this cast for about a day, did I realize: I forgot Jesus.

I forgot the Christ child.

The centerpiece of the entire story. The reason for the New Testament. The culmination of two thousand years of waiting and prophecy and hope and despair. The Light that broke into the darkness. And I forgot to include him in the cast of characters.

This stuns me with shame. I want to turn my back on myself and walk away, shaking my head as I lock the office and turn in my keys.

But isn't this the way it works so often in our society? We try so hard to get to Christmas Day: deck the halls, buy the gifts, wrap the gifts, and try not to deck everyone who gets in the way. We dare to dream that we might find the perfect something for someone who really needs something perfect. We nibble our lips and scrunch our eyes in our concern for others' experience of Christmas.

Perhaps we hope, too, that someone else will find the perfect something for us, something that will prove they love us, they'd been thinking of us, that they have an inside line into our secret hopes and dreams.

We hurtle through the entire holiday season, sometimes almost panting in the race. We chug up to the finish line: tree trimmed, gifts wrapped, everybody happy sitting around the tree. (Oh wait, was that just a movie we watched? Because how often is that the real story?) And then the hollowness clangs inside of us, a dissonant, empty gonging. Because this wasn't, after all, what we sought, craved, dreamed of for Christmas Day.

Advent means "coming," and it is this coming that we seek. The coming of Emmanuel foretold by Isaiah (7:14) into all of our hurtling, chugging, mind-numbing discouragement. The light of Christ streaming into our tattered darkness, the gloom of depression, and the haze of broken dreams and shattered relationships.

The Wonderful Counselor, Mighty God, Everlasting Father, Prince of Peace—how our backs ache for the one who will carry the government on his shoulders (see Isa. 9:6–7).

If this describes your journey, your hope, this is the right place. You are not alone. Because Advent is about all of us— all of our situations: the brokenhearted, the barren, the aged, the young, the pregnant teenager and her disillusioned fiancé, the faithful, the doubting, the people who go through the motions of faith even though faced with God's silence. Poverty and power, wealth and worry, hope and heartbreak, oppression and opulence.

And always the movement of God propels events forward— all these characters from different times and places prophesying Christ's advent and reminding us to watch and hope. Words echo from as far back as Eden ("He will crush your head," God said to the serpent in Gen. 3:15) and finally, after all this waiting, God's words break into time.

One more thing about the participants in the advent: the story rolls along without an appearance from the main character until well into the drama, as the last scene in the last act draws near. But the focus of all the activity in the advent narratives was Christ, not the people's agendas in the last days of B.C. time. Because the people's agendas were about Christ, and all their activities prepared the way for him.

He was the anticipated guest every single day. For the fifteen or more months from the angel's announcement to Zechariah all the way to the birth in Bethlehem, Christ was the unseen motivator.

At this child's birth—this juxtaposition of heaven entering earth and lordship born on a cold dirt floor—the axis of time shifted to before and after. The King of Glory came wrapped in rags, lying in a trough, born of a mother in the usual way of kings and peasants alike, but unlike any who came before or who have come since. This child entered earthly time, God's fullness into humanity's taut limits.

What do we want for Christmas? Maybe Christmas isn't about getting what we think we want. Maybe it's about getting what we need, and then realizing, once we open the gift, that what we need is actually what we wanted all along.

Imagine God saying these words over you, right now:

> Dear one,
> Don't worry about the calendar
> And don't worry about the clock.
> Forget about the lists.
> Your lists,
> Others' lists,
> Your forgiveness lists,
> And your unforgiveness lists.
> Every year
> You try so hard,
> But really
> Only one thing
> Is needed.
> Come to me
> Sit by me.
> I have a story
> To tell you
> About a time

And a place
And a people
Who needed
To be found in the dark.
Don't worry,
I have a light.
I am the light.
I am sending the Light
Of the world.

Perhaps you can join me in this prayer: "OK, God. I'm quitting right now. Quitting my list-making, my driven-ness, putting it all aside. I'm ready to hear the story all over again, with new ears. Speak, please, into the darkness, and bring your light. Amen."

This Advent, may God fulfill all of our hopes and dreams with the Gift we've been waiting for all our lives.

WEEK 1 OF ADVENT

1

HIGH RISK ADVENT-URE

The First Sunday of Advent

The Word became flesh and made his dwelling among us.

—JOHN 1:14

Advent seems like a risky act on God's part. Imagine creating a world and giving everyone in it the same opportunity to love or forsake the Creator. And then, after people thoroughly botched their opportunity to enjoy God's presence, imagine God establishing hundreds of rules about right living. The rules helped people live their daily lives so that they could enter a relationship with a holy God. Those rules made sense if the most important one was, "Love the Lord your God with all your heart and with all your soul and with all your strength" (Deut. 6:5). Imagine, too, that some of those rules included consequences for sin and thus entailed judgment.

And then, consider that God created those laws, carved the top ten with a holy hand into stone, and then passed them on to Moses on the mountain, who passed them on to the people, who promptly and regularly broke them. Consider that God knew this breakdown would happen. The Creator absolutely knew from day one of creation that there was only one way to bring people back into relationship with himself. And so the adventure called Advent began at the very beginning, confounding our common sense, our logic, our reason. *National Geographic*, MapQuest, our moral compasses, and our thinking caps could never divine the route for such an adventure.

Advent broke social taboos established and carefully handed down.

For instance, an engaged woman found guilty of adultery was subject to stoning (see Lev. 20:10; Deut. 22:20–24). Her fiancé or parents had every right to turn her over to the establishment to see justice met, unless the man chose to marry her. Mary's story of a divine conception could well have been construed as a teenager's ruse to escape the consequences due anyone who committed adultery.

And another example: Old Testament interpretation considered barren women to be suffering the consequences of their own sin, with barrenness being one of the curses God said would follow people for their unfaithfulness. If children were a heritage from the Lord, and "blessed is the man whose quiver is full," then the lack thereof was the same as the withdrawal of God's kindness, as absence of blessing, punishment for sin (see Ex. 23:25–26; Ps. 127:3–5).

Spoiler alert: In the advent, God confounded expectations and declared holy an act that appeared to deserve the death penalty or at least societal censure. And just like at creation, God again granted people, these failure-prone creations, the right to accept or reject his arrival.

The super-sized *risk* of the advent fits perfectly the word it grew into: *adventure*. Yes, the advent meant a wonder, a miracle, accounts of marvelous things. But it also meant risk, danger, taking a chance, a perilous undertaking. Advent, anyone? For isn't adventure the centerpiece of this coming?

God took a chance; God risked everything; God set up a wonder, a miracle, a host of marvelous things in the advent. In this great adventure, heaven first entered earth in the form of an angel, interrupting the regularly scheduled program of disaster, despair, and darkness and declaring good news to a sad man nearing retirement who never gave up. Light broke into the bleakness of a woman's barrenness, hope swallowed up unhappiness. Soon, another angel appeared to a humble girl. Angels sang, shepherds quaked, kings brought gifts, evil rulers were thwarted, and life overshadowed death. Wombs were filled, and dreams, prayers, and promises were fulfilled, and . . . and at last—at last—the great chasm between heaven and earth was bridged by the One sent from eternity: the One who came, who comes, who will come again.

This adventure produced a brilliant musical extravaganza: the pageantry of angels hovering in the night sky and a star lighting the path for others to follow; the pathos of an unmarried teenager who stepped into a role no one would want to audition for but who carried her part with a song in her heart.

This adventure, this advent, delivers people from darkness into light, sets prisoners free, lifts up the downtrodden, and binds the wounds of the brokenhearted. This advent takes people in all their brokenness, all their disappointment and sorrow, and in a divine twist invites them into the adventure, the adventure that brings the Divine into a long-waiting world.

In advent, God comes to earth and welcomes us to heaven in a holy mystery beyond words or reason. In advent, God chases us down, coming after us to bring us back.

Magnificent God inhabiting human frailty, the God of the universe in the body of a baby. Dare we say, "Welcome"? As though we could stop this miracle, as though in some way we can inhibit that coming, whether by our flat disbelief, our rational mind, or just the tattered way we try to weave our lives together on the loom of this world.

When we find the Messiah, we find both the beginning of our greatest adventure and the fulfillment of our greatest desire.

And what do we say to this? What can we possibly say?

Let the adventure begin.

REFLECTION

In what ways do you experience Advent as adventure? What do you consider risky, daring, about God's adventure from heaven to earth, and our adventure from earth to heaven? What risk do you take coming to Advent this season?

BENEDICTION

Dear one,
At last, at last,
The light shines
In all the dark places
And mystery replaces misery
And rules collapse
And the reign of the One
Who has waited since eternity past begins.
Incense and angels,
Dreams and prophesies,

Heaven reaches earth,
And hope turns to reality.
The adventure begins.
And you are the reason.
So buckle up
And hold tight
Because the scenes
You are about to enter
Will challenge everything
You believed
And fulfill everything
You ever hoped for.
Welcome aboard.
Let the Advent begin.

PRAYER

God, you took a risk coming for *me* in this way. I want to say yes to this Advent, to this adventure, today, and in these coming days. Help me to see your coming, to experience your coming, to live in accordance with your coming, and to hasten your coming once again.

2

IN THOSE DAYS

The people walking in darkness have seen a great light;
on those living in the land of deep darkness a light has dawned.

—ISAIAH 9:2

It was in "the time of Herod king of Judea," Luke 1:5 tells us. Darkness stretched through generations, the darkness of waiting for hope on the horizon. For four hundred years, they watched, they waited. Some abandoned their posts on the crows' nests of their souls. Some decided perhaps God wasn't serious after all about that guarantee of a deliverer, that Root of Jesse, the heir to King David's throne.

People waited in the long silence, the dearth of words from a God who maybe no longer cared or longed to deliver them. Perhaps, some concluded, God isn't really God. Some gave God a small *g*, had a little fling with other small-*g* gods, and decided to go about their business as though long-ago promises no longer mattered. Promises of salvation. Promises of a king to deliver them from the oppression, taxation, and dreadful dull boredom of a world with its soul shuttered, all the lights gone out in the big house on the hill.

And given the reign of the current king, "King Herod the Great" as some referenced him, . . . well, *great* might have been overstating the case, at least in terms of this man's character and stability. Maybe he nicknamed himself. Though a brilliant architect, he careened wildly between Great Paranoiac and Great Madman, Great Zealot and Great Brownnoser. He murdered some of his own family members and reportedly sent out secret police to eavesdrop to learn his ranking in the popularity polls. Rumor has it that public dissenters sometimes just disappeared, and this despot enforced a gag order against public protests to protect his great ego.

King Herod couldn't decide which side of the fence to claim, since both the Jewish and the Gentile sides had political and popular merit, so he tried to curry favor with the Jews by giving attention to their temple. It perhaps seemed a minor concession to Jewish interests. Years after the destruction of King Solomon's original temple, the Jewish exiles had returned from Babylon to repair and rebuild it, directed by Nehemiah. That only took four decades. By the time Herod entered the picture, the now-dilapidated building needed serious help again. He decided to hire the priests and rebuild and embellish the temple for yet another forty-year renovation. By the time he finished, the temple was glorious, absolutely transformed, unrecognizable from its former state. Then Herod, figuring he'd pleased the Jews plenty, opted to improve his standing in the polls with Gentiles, so he brought in priests from Babylonia and Alexandria to help run the Jewish temple. Naturally, polluting the temple with paganism did *wonders* for his popularity with the Jews.

The Jewish people groaned under chaotic leadership, injustice, and heavy taxation. The darkness of poverty and a poor economy eroded their fragile foundation of hope for relief, for some flicker of light on the horizon.

Is it so different today in our lives, in our world?

This waiting shrouds us in darkness—the darkness of doubt, when hope sustains a hairline fracture, an underground fault line that might activate and split the world into pieces at any moment. It is a darkness, perhaps, with which we are all familiar. Broken dreams, broken promises, broken hearts, all in shattered fragments like remnants from old bottles used in target practice. The shards of our hopes scatter around our feet, making it hard for us to shift our stance, let alone walk forward in this world.

Into this dark waiting, Luke writes to us. In this bleak season of our lives—for don't we hope (there's that word again) that it is merely a season in life, not the definition of our entire life?—in this thickness, we hear, for the first time or the thousandth time, the beginnings of the story. Or, if not the beginning, certainly the continuation of the strains heard long ago, a refrain heard throughout all the days of God's creation.

This dreary epoch feels so personal and private, yet we find this season peopled with a cast of characters on a stage the size of the world. Into this season we hear the words anew: "The people walking in darkness have seen a great light."

REFLECTION

Where is it dark for you right now? Who are the people in your life who sit in darkness?

BENEDICTION

Dear one,
You've been sitting
There in the dark
For too long,
The shards of life
Broken about your feet,
Your relationships tattered
And hopes shattered.
But wait with me here.
Hope is on the horizon
Because the sun is rising
And the Son,
My Son,
Is coming.

PRAYER

In spite of it all, in spite of all the fractures around me and in me, I will wait, God. This season, I will watch and wait. And hope. Don't give up on me. And please, don't let me give up.

3

NO ORDINARY TOUR OF DUTY

Once when Zechariah's division was on duty and he was serving
as priest before God, he was chosen by lot, according to the custom
of the priesthood, to go into the temple of the Lord and burn
incense. And when the time for the burning of incense came
all the assembled worshipers were praying outside.

—LUKE 1:8–10

Once, a long time ago, there was priest named Zechariah.
His name meant, "God remembers," yet how many days had
he awakened with disappointment clogging his throat and
short-circuiting his faith? How could he believe, after all his
years, perhaps some fifty-odd, that God remembered him
personally? Hadn't Zechariah shown up day after day for his
entire life; kept the commandments; and put up with crooked,
elite priests who demanded such coddling that the rest of the
priests had to take on day jobs, in spite of God's commandments
that they be provided for? A man's insurance policy in those
days consisted of children, and since Zechariah didn't have a
son to care for him in his old age, he likely worked double duty
as both priest and farmer.

And where was God when he really needed him? Years of
waiting, trying to be faithful, the legal people adding all sorts
of additional rules to keep people toeing the line and hoeing
the row, and here, after years of observance, all Zechariah had
to show for it was a barren wife and an empty nursery thick

with cobwebs. Maybe some days he wasn't so sure which he wanted more, a child or the Messiah, and other days, he clamped down on all hopes and just did his job. He swallowed his discouragement, though it was like gulping down sand.

In all the divisions, as many as twenty thousand priests served among the people, so Zechariah's entire division handled temple duty probably only a couple of times a year, for a week at a stretch. And one day, out of his eight-hundred-some division compatriots, Zechariah's straw was drawn. At last, at last, this one day in his life, he won; *he* got to enter the temple and burn the incense, just like Aaron all those centuries before him (Ex. 30:7–8).

The people assembled outside, worshiping. Zechariah, this man named "God Remembers," entered the Holy Place, just outside the Holy of Holies. Had his heart jumped into his mouth, making it hard to worship, think, or even breathe? His sole role was to enter, cast the incense onto the altar, prostrate himself, and then leave.

That was it. A lifetime of waiting, all that buildup of anticipation, and it would be over in mere minutes. His fifteen seconds of fame. If it went on too long, the people outside would grow anxious, restless, wondering if the priest who drew the lot also got his number called and died in there. That was an impertinent place to die, so priests probably tried to avoid that. It might hurt one's reputation, like maybe God had struck him down deader than last year's flowers from the altar guild.

This day, this once-in-a-lifetime, "come-on-down" moment, Zechariah gathered his robes about him and entered. And there it was. The altar—acacia wood overlaid with gold—glowing, last night's incense ready to be replaced, the embers desperate for a new touch of fire. How he must have sighed, entering at last, trying to remember that God remembers, that God surely was coming soon, that the advent was drawing near.

No matter what will happen next, no matter what hasn't happened before—in Zechariah's life, my life, in your life—what occurs at this junction in the story is this: we remember that God remembers. Maybe we run through our own list of disappointments, the deep darkness that afflicts us from time to time, that sludge we try to sidestep or forget entirely. Yet this is the "God remembers" season, these days of Advent. The world around us might forget; and sometimes we forget, too, in our rushing about and in all the holiday expectations and traumas. But God remembers.

He remembers the disappointment. Remembers the painful journey to get to this day in our lives. Remembers all those pleas, and the please-and-thank-yous, too. Remembers the politics that detour us, the unfulfilling jobs, the hopes we pinned on something or someone only to have them vaporize like steam blowing out of street vents on a winter's day of our soul.

Here it was, this normal day, and here Zechariah was, this normal man, going about his normal job. And here we are, too.

And the miracle is that God remembers.

REFLECTION

What do you try to forget, early in this season? What do you remember? What do you hope God remembers as you enter Advent? What do you hope God forgets?

BENEDICTION

Dear one,
I remember.
I cannot forget you;
You are engraved on my hands,
Tattooed on my heart.
I've been watching out for you
And watching for you
Every day of your life.
I remember your pain;
I know your disappointments,
Your sadness,
All the almosts and not-quites
Of your life.
I see how you show up,
Trying to be faithful,
To cover all the bases before you,
And that sometimes, oftentimes,
There's not enough of you to go around
And you can't get everything done.
And here's the truth:
I rejoice in you
No matter what.
But in this season of "I remember,"
You remember, too:
In your normal day,
Your normal job,
I am with you.

PRAYER

I remember, God, the things I want to forget, and forget the things—and the people and the goodness and you—that I really, really want to remember. Thank you for not forgetting me, for remembering me. Make this time a Holy Place, and let my time with you be sweet incense.

THE BIG QUESTION

Zechariah . . . belonged to the priestly division of Abijah; his wife
Elizabeth was also a descendant of Aaron. Both of them were
righteous in the sight of God, observing all the Lord's commands
and decrees blamelessly. But they were childless, because
Elizabeth was not able to conceive; and they were both very old.

—LUKE 1:5–7

Zechariah, descendent of Aaron, hailed from a long lineage
of priests who sought to be faithful. But who of them had no
children? Zechariah wouldn't have existed if there'd been
barrenness in just one generation before him. So his very
presence testified of God's faithfulness.

Why, then, this apparent lapse in that faithfulness,
Zechariah's lack of children? Did he enter the Holy Place,
asking, pleading for answers? Because surely he carried his
own agenda into that place, even as he also carried his
responsibilities and authority as a priest.

It is the darkest of dark, this sense of annihilation, of being
forgotten, of not mattering. Isn't that the bottom line for all of
us? At times, it seems as though we just don't exist and don't
matter. Part of the deep cry of our souls is that we want our
presence on this planet to make a difference. It isn't just about
being noticed either; it's also about being cared for.

This man, from generations of men who shared such
desires, entered the advent story as a man who was "righteous

in the sight of God, observing all the Lord's commands and decrees blamelessly" (Luke 1:6). *All* is quite a word, given the vast number of rules it entailed. Still, Zechariah showed up and kept doing the right next thing.

Zechariah's sort of waiting convicts me in a world that carries the subtext, "You owe me . . . right now." We don't wait for God—or anyone else for that matter—to provide. We go into debt or substitute other things or people for our real dream. Isn't this a subtle type of annihilation, a submission to foreign rule and even oppression? We live in the land of plenty, yet we still want plenty more, and it enslaves us. Maybe in some secret closet of our soul, we even think that God owes us because we've been trying so hard in such difficult times, but God doesn't ante up. So we quit showing up, quit praying, quit playing the Christian "game," and give up on God. Because God isn't answering.

And is it ever dark!

Zechariah kept the faith. He didn't allow his disappointment to lead to disobedience. How astounding, to continue walking faithfully in spite of such darkness. How did he stay present—to his wife, Elizabeth, to his priestly duties, to his relationships in the town and at his day job—and hold back the creeping, sweeping tide of bitterness and resentment?

Maybe there's a secret to faithfulness in dark times experienced while awaiting some long-promised but obscure light, even a light you know might not occur in your lifetime: focus on a deeper reality than the visible darkness—the darkness of oppression, of a rotted economy and a maniac despot for a ruler, and of foreign occupation. After all, isn't this the situation in much of the world today? And isn't this darkness visible in our private and public lives, with our struggles, unmet expectations, and hopes? The light hidden behind the clouds of our daily lives and the dark nights of our soul is the "sunrise from on high." And one thing about the sun: it always rises.

We just have to wait. And watch. Because here's the truth: God is as faithful as the sun. And Advent? Advent means God sent the Son, the Son is coming.

REFLECTION

What do you really need during this season? To be noticed? To have a long-held prayer answered? To know that God knows you?

BENEDICTION

Dear one,
Of course you have an agenda.
And though it might surprise you,
I am not surprised
By your long-held wants and dreams
Or by your disappointments and disillusionments.
But watch the light
Not the night.
Watch that morning sky.
Because I gild every day
With my faithfulness.

PRAYER

Help me to focus, God, on who you are and not just what you do, or don't do, in my life or in this world. Help me see your faithfulness and presence in my life.

5

OUT OF THE DARKNESS

Then an angel of the Lord appeared to him, standing
at the right side of the altar of incense. When Zechariah
saw him, he was startled and was gripped with fear.

—LUKE 1:11–12

Dark silence stretched like thick black curtains, silence so deep the philosophers surely started a new chant, some version of the "God is dead" line that rolls into our culture during difficult times. Into that sort of silence sneaks a dread, a fear, that God has forgotten, that God doesn't care, and it is like tearing earth out of its gravitational pull and flinging it out into the universe. To live without certainty that God is alive, that God cares, is to live unmoored, unhinged, with all the doors and windows of our souls flapping in a tornado.

Zechariah entered the Holy Place and, his first time in, he thought he knew what to expect. Others would have told him, perhaps, detailing the area: the special wood, the gold overlays, the candle stands. But they described a room. To depict what Zechariah saw is a wordless endeavor, beyond any wild imaginings for a grounded priest. There, to the right of the altar, stood an angel. We can't see the angel's face, don't know how tall he is, what he looks like, what he's wearing, if he has wings. Nothing.

Zechariah's reaction tells us enough: startled. He about jumped out of his skin. Then: fear. Fear embraced him, wrapped its tentacles about him, and pressed down on him.

After years, decades, lifetimes of silence, through this visitor, the God of all the earth broke into time, into Zechariah's very personal time. God sent an angel to speak. And the angel's first words, this messenger of God?

"Do not fear."

The angel's words come to us, too, in the dark, in the creeping silence that feels like God's absence. For our fear is our unmentionable; our fear is what we don't talk about in church. Our fear is also our shame, which keeps our jaws clamped together and keeps us awake at night. We aren't supposed to be afraid, but we are.

The angel told the priest, there in the room wrapped with gold, "Do not be afraid, Zechariah, Mr. 'God Remembers.' Do not be afraid." I need those words to be almost physical—to clutch in my hand, to pull out and read and ingest, to put on a watch fob and help me tell time by them. Because behind those four words is the timeless truth that God is on duty. God has us covered, has our backs.

But the assurance comes next; this isn't just a platitude, something a doctor murmurs over us or a mother whispers as she rocks a child after a nightmare.

"Do not be afraid, Zechariah; your prayer has been heard."

What prayer? What was he talking about? Your prayer . . . singular? *The* prayer, the great desire, the one thing Zechariah wanted more than anything else? And now we know the truth. We know what beat on this man's heart every single day for so many years, all the years he kept the faith and honored his vows. The angel's words tell us.

"Your wife Elizabeth will bear you a son, and you will give him the name John" (Luke 1:13 NASB).

And the answer to a lifetime of prayer, to a culture's expectation, poured over Zechariah, as golden as the glow on the altar. God's promise through the angel continued, but Zechariah barely stemmed the flood of questions bubbling up until the angel fell silent again, prophecy completed.

Then Zechariah's words flash-flooded, words he probably wished for months later he could swallow. "How can I be sure of this? I am an old man and my wife is well along in years" (Luke 1:18). Zechariah knew the impossibility of this prediction, even though he also knew his people's history. He knew the age of the woman's womb meant nothing to God. Look at Sarah, the great-grandmother of millions of people. Hadn't she been without a child until in her nineties? Intellectually, this priest knew that nothing was impossible with God. Just unlikely.

Miracles, after all, don't happen to us personally; we hear about them in others' lives, other places, other times. We read about them in magazines or blogs, or see them in movies. Besides, God isn't a genie in a lamp granting wishes. We know this. Plenty of couples have been unable to bear children, and God didn't send an angel to announce the answer to their prayers.

This makes me squirm, knowing that God remembers and also that God might not work it out in our lives like Zechariah's. But regardless of the outcome, isn't the angel's word to us the same? "Do not be afraid." Because God remembers.

REFLECTION

How do you handle another's miracle? Even if you don't tell anyone but God, what is your largest single prayer request? How do the waiting and the nonanswer impact your deepest, yet-unanswered prayer? To your soul?

BENEDICTION

Dear one,
You think I don't remember,
But I never forget anything.
Not your hopes,
Not your dreams,
Not your prayers
In the middle of the night
And in the light of day.
I remember,
And I see.
Don't forget
That I remember;
And don't forget
That I will not fail.
My compassions never fail.
Watch for them.
Watch for me.
With all that said,
The angel is right—
I hear you.

PRAYER

God, I confess it's easy to give up hope or to look with envy on another's blessings. But if you remember me, then I have all I need.

6

GOD SPOKE; ZECHARIAH WENT SILENT

And now you will be silent.

—LUKE 1:20

The angel waited for Zechariah's question, Zechariah's doubt, to splay out in the Holy Place. Waited for Zechariah to realize what he'd just revealed about himself: "How can I know this for sure?" Zechariah dared to ask for a sign from the angel? Was he impatient after so many years of praying, possibly even praying without any hope of an answer?

This seems especially daring, and also shortsighted, because when we're talking about having babies, we can know for sure within a few short—or long—months if the process worked. So even if Zechariah's question was just rusty water seeping from an old pipe, we can assume he knew the drill.

Maybe Zechariah's question wasn't about the obvious; the angel had delivered a mouthful of promises to him, far more than just "You will have a child."

This child would be the long-awaited forerunner to the Messiah, the one who would prepare the way, make rough roads smooth, and call out in the wilderness, "Make way!" This child would have the spirit and power of Elijah.

This child, this long-awaited child, would do far more than either Zechariah or Elizabeth, his long-suffering wife, could have asked for or imagined.

And, even if they can't verbalize it, isn't that the deep longing of parents' hearts? Don't parents want their children to far surpass their own limitations and giftings, to exceed finite parental imaginings? As we come to know God, we realize that the world around us is only a fragment of the big picture, that in the world beyond the tangible, heavenly things happen. This surely is an unspoken desire of all parents' hearts: that their children make a difference. That heavenly things might happen in and through them.

So perhaps Zechariah's question, "How can I know this for sure?" was greater than just a simple stuttering of disbelief. The question tapped into his deepest longing, maybe more than he realized.

But that's not all: "I'm an old man, and my wife far along in years." Is it possible that the question wasn't about actually giving birth, about how this could happen since his wife likely was in menopause, or about the hopes harbored for his child? But instead about whether Zechariah and his wife would live long enough to prove out the prophecy? To have a child is miraculous. To have one at the priest's age and stage was even more so. To have a child who filled the holy sandals the angel laid out for him was almost beyond belief. To live to see beyond the baby's childhood would allow Zechariah to see the prophecy confirmed. And perhaps we're back to the root of the question: Zechariah's trust that the prophecy was from God. "How can I be certain?"

But the angel knew. As silence fell into that Holy Place, as Zechariah dared to look into the angel's face, the angel introduced himself.

"I am Gabriel. I stand in the presence of God" (Luke 1:19).

Gabriel, one of seven archangels who we later learn stand in the presence of God (see Rev. 1:4). Gabriel who appeared to Daniel to explain a horrifying vision of the end times (Dan. 8:16–27), the explanation of which rendered Daniel ill for days. *That* angel. If Zechariah weren't already terrified, that should about do him in, right there in the Holy Place. Gabriel's next words to Zechariah contained both a chastisement and a gift. "And now you will be silent and unable to speak until the day this happens, because you did not believe my words" (Luke 1:20).

God broke the centuries-long silence with the angel's words and revealed the doubt hidden in the dark void of generations. And then God reintroduced silence from the earthly end of the wire, shutting down Zechariah's words for nearly a year.

Those long months meant the priest must watch and process rather than comment or interject. For Elizabeth's pregnancy, he was unable to "Use your words" as parents tell their children. The silence invited him to feel, to notice and cherish. Silence forced him to listen—to his wife, to the world, to God's work. Silence allowed him to savor the miracle unfolding in front of his wait-dulled eyes. The quiet moved him deeper, creating a holy place within his soul. In that wordless space, maybe he began to experience what it meant to be loved.

Finding Life
Jane Rubietta

wesleyan.org/wph

"Jane unearths the roots that connect us to the gardens of Eden and Gethsemane, revealing God's transformational garden-work for our souls."

—Bishop Jonathon Keaton

. . . .

Jane Rubietta is the critically acclaimed author of numerous books and articles. Jane brings a voice of vulnerability, hope, and humor as she writes and speaks on issues close to people's hearts.

For more information about Jane and her speaking schedule, visit janerubietta.com

. . . .

Find **Jane Rubietta** and complimentary resources for her books online at wphonline.com

Without his tongue flapping, perhaps he acknowledged his own lack of faith that showed up inconveniently during his once-in-a-lifetime moment in the Holy Place. How he must have regretted that his doubts revealed his true self, his disbelief, his lack of faith. There he was, a priest, after all. How shame must have twined its roots around his mind and heart, strangling him.

Silence gave him time to sort through that shame, to move to a place of deeper belief and trust. Time to listen and love. And the shame became gain, transforming him into a man through whom God would continue to speak.

REFLECTION

Nine months is a pretty long silent retreat. What if you tried, during Advent, to be silent for five minutes a day? Just quiet the words, doubts, and flyaway brain, and keep coming back to God. What is this like for you? What scares you or worries you about silence?

BENEDICTION

Dear one,
How much better
If you would believe first
And question never.
Ah, but you will have doubts.
And if you can stop
And listen to my longing for you,
Then even your doubts become a holy place,
Because there you meet me
Again.
There you listen

Again.
There you learn to love
Again.
So feel free to doubt,
But in your doubt
Do not turn away from me.
I will turn your shame to gain.

PRAYER

God, help me to trust you this Advent—trust that your loving timing will be adequate in my life, trust that you will do what you have promised, trust that you hear the longings of my heart. And help me to be quiet, to wait for your coming, so that I can notice you.

7

RECOGNITION

When [Zechariah] came out, he could not speak to them.
They realized he had seen a vision in the temple,
for he kept making signs to them.

—LUKE 1:22

Outside the temple, the people fidgeted, restless and worried. They'd finished their prayers long ago. Why hadn't the priest returned? Had God struck him dead? Had the coals flamed into a conflagration and the incense exploded? We can only assume, but don't even know from the Scriptures, that Zechariah actually got the incense lit.

But when Zechariah finally appeared, didn't his face tell a story that his words couldn't? Surely his face glowed from a heavenly encounter. Surely after this miracle encounter in the Holy Place, his entire countenance changed, like Moses after seeing God up on the mountain and needing to veil his face on the way downhill so the people didn't get sunburned. "They realized he had seen a vision," Luke tells us. It was obvious. He couldn't talk. He used hand gestures. He had to watch people closely to see if they understood his sign language and his scribblings.

"They realized he had seen a vision." Because we can tell, can't we, if people have been with God, have been in the

Holy Place, have been touched by God? We can tell by their demeanor, by their actions and gestures, by their words. Or even by the profound kindness and depth of their accepting silences. Some of the deepest, most influential people I know are men and women who do not need to talk incessantly, but who listen at a level of stillness that translates as love and empathy. And in the midst of Advent, isn't this also the breaking of the light into the darkness of the world?

As sure as the sun breaks through the curtain of night and pours across the horizon, so do our acts of love and attentiveness split the nighttime of discouragement and despondency, and speak of a love greater than this world can even contain.

Advent is a difficult season, partly because of the hoopla and fa-la-la drummed up by marketing geniuses, the glittering faux overlay we have come to expect in our own holiday traditions and trimmings. But it is also spiritually flat sometimes, because contemplating a baby's birth becomes a little obscure, really, even if all the events leading up to that birth are spectacular, even if they fulfill prophecy after prophecy given since the beginning of time. And if we hear the same message, year after year after year, then doesn't it lose its special quality?

But what if the amazing truth about Advent is that the Light came into the world and the world could not, absolutely could not, despite all its darkest efforts, extinguish it? Didn't Jesus say, "I am the light of the world," (John 8:12) and then, "You are the light of the world" (Matt. 5:14)? And what if one amazing application of Advent is that the Light now lives in us, and we open our mouths, hands, and hearts and light pours out? What if that kind of glory happened day after day, and we deliberately sought to convey light to the people around us? "Let your light so shine," Jesus said (Matt. 5:16 KJV).

Sometimes in my hurry to get in and get out of a store during Christmas shopping, I forget to even meet the eyes of the check-out people. The trip is all about me, even if the gift is for someone else. Both the haste and lack of eye contact are about my needs, schedule, or issues—my self-preoccupation.

But when I do meet someone's eye, read the nametag, greet that person by name, and smile with recognition that says, "I know you; you're just like me; you have pain; you are tired; and this is supposed to be a holiday season, and I'm sad that your life is hard," then kindness creates an arc of electricity between us. People just want to be noticed, really; for someone to say, "I see you; you matter; your pain and problems matter; and I am grateful you are part of this world."

Isn't this why Christ came, really? To bridge the dark gap between us, between ourselves and others, and others and God. To say, with God, "I see you; you matter; and I am bringing you the best gift possible: my love, my forgiveness, my hope."

Like the people fidgeting outside the temple, may others know we have been with God and see Christ coming. Through us.

REFLECTION

When do you experience Christ coming into your day, your life? What happens that helps you to recognize his coming, his advent? When do you recognize Christ saying, "I see you. You matter. Here's my love for you"? And how, or when, or do you, convey that light into others' darkness? When have people noticed that you have been with God?

BENEDICTION

Dear one,
I do see you.
I see you through the eyes of my Son,
The One who came to save you,
To remind you and prove to you
That you matter.
And when you see another through my eyes,
Through the eyes of my Son,
They will see Christmas;
They will see Advent;
They will know the arc of kindness
That comes from being recognized
And appreciated
And given a name.
Look deeply;
Forgive quickly;
Love well;
Open your life to others.
In doing so,
You bring the sun into their darkness
And the Son into their world.

PRAYER

God, come to me, come through me, into this world. Help me to notice others, to love them as though they are already friends and family. Bring your light through me into their darkness this season.

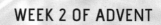

WEEK 2 OF ADVENT

8

FROM BARREN TO BLESSED

The Second Sunday of Advent

Both of them were righteous in the sight of God, observing
all the Lord's commands and decrees blamelessly. But they were
childless because Elizabeth was unable to conceive.

—LUKE 1:6–7

No doubt both Elizabeth and Zechariah knew the psalm that God "settles the childless woman in her home as a happy mother of children" (113:9). And they absolutely knew the stories of the founding families of their faith: Of Abraham and Sarah, who conceived in their nineties after decades of barrenness. Of infertile Rachel, sick with jealousy of her sister Leah; beautiful, spoiled Rachel, who gripped her husband Jacob's lapels and cried out, "Give me children, or I'll die!" (Gen. 30:1). Of Hannah, who prayed forever for a son, and the other wife, Peninnah, whose fertility made Hannah's life miserable. Zechariah and Elizabeth knew how God finally and dramatically answered the prayers of all these brokenhearted couples.

But Sarah, in her impatience to conceive, threw in the towel on waiting and tossed her hat into the ring of competition, convincing Abraham to have a relationship with Hagar. The animosity between Abraham's two sons, half-brothers, continues in their families to this day. On another branch of the family tree, Rachel threw her maid at Jacob to make babies in her impatience to have children in her own time, just like her husband's grandmother, Sarah.

Because people saw children as the Lord's blessing, they assumed barrenness was the opposite, a curse for unfaithfulness. Jacob answered Rachel's begging with, "Am I in the place of God, who has kept you from having children?" (see Gen. 30:2).

Luke highlights the uprightness of Zechariah and Elizabeth so that we are clear: the couple's inability to conceive was not due to sin, nor did it lead them to sin. Barrenness didn't woo them to unfaithfulness. No second wives or mistresses or backup plan. And no tossing in the towel on their faith, either. They didn't leave God because God hadn't acted as they expected. Zechariah and Elizabeth didn't use their disappointment as a reason to sin, to stray from the path of righteousness. Couldn't they have used the excuse, "I deserve this excess, this detour into sin, this illicit reward, because life has been hard, or God has been unfair, or . . ."?

Both Zechariah and Elizabeth figured out how to live good, obedient lives in spite of their disappointment, in spite of their great heart's desire being unfulfilled. They didn't turn bitter, turn against God, or flat-out embrace a flagrant lifestyle of sin. Their uprightness serves like a megaphone amplifying their character, given the 613 laws in the Torah they were expected to obey.

They didn't disobey, nor did they release their grip on hope, as we see from the angel's words: "Your prayer has been answered." They continued to pray in spite of all the discouraging evidence to the contrary, all the statistics that preclude conceiving after age fifty, everything that suggested that God didn't give two hoots about their longings, that God had actually even forgotten the promise to send the Messiah.

Barrenness is not simply a female issue, women unable to bear children. For each of us, men and women alike, it is the infertile soil of brokenness. Broken hopes—the tree trunks of fruitless dreams. Broken promises—others' promises to us and our promises to others. Promises seemingly broken by God to us, or at least, not fulfilled in the way we expected, wanted, or felt we deserve. The emptiness that comes from living with darkness for far too long. The empty womb of our soul, not life-giving to us or to others.

The barrenness of all our disappointments—the abuse, pain, sorrow, and just plain old difficulties of living in this world. The barrenness of empty jobs, meaningless, rote work day in and day out; unfulfilling tasks; and awkward, disappointing, or nonexistent relationships. Barrenness that results from not knowing or not using our gifts, or not having those gifts and uniquenesses acknowledged or welcomed. Barrenness from not finding a spot where we fit in this world.

Ultimately, barrenness is the sense that our lives don't make a difference. That our presence in this world is irrelevant. That, unlike fruitful people, we leave no legacy behind us when the shades are drawn on our lives.

Advent, this adventure, confronts and converts all that fruitlessness through words spoken in an inner room about a son who would "go on before the Lord . . . to turn the hearts of the parents to their children and the disobedient to the wisdom of the righteous—to make ready a people prepared for the Lord" (Luke 1:17).

Advent comes into their world and says, "This is grace that goes before, grace that prepares the way for others to receive the coming Christ."

Advent comes into our world, as well. Regardless of our age, our stage in life, the job we have or don't have, or other life matters, we prepare the way for the Anointed One, the One named "God is our salvation," "God with us."

We live straight-up lives, like signs that always point to God. We trust even when the world is dark, because we know that in God's doings, night is finite. Elizabeth and Zechariah's lives were the means by which God prepared people for the Messiah, and his desire to use individual lives has never ever changed. God will take our obedience and barrenness and prepare others for the Messiah. It's a miracle.

REFLECTION

Where do you feel fruitless or barren? When do you give up hope and quit praying? When do you give in to discouragement and stray? Where have you seen fruit in ways different from or beyond your prayers?

BENEDICTION

Dear one,
Do not let the darkness
Persuade you that I am not
On your side.
Do not let your feelings of barrenness,
The lack of fruitfulness and meaning,

Hinder your coming to me
With your brokenness,
All those promises,
Those hurts,
Those losses.
Because I hear you;
I hear your words,
Though you feel mute,
And I always have fruit
Planned for you.
So come to me
In the dark,
And I promise
The light will shine
In you,
Through you,
And you will leave your mark—
My mark—
On this world.

PRAYER

God, I bring my frustration over the lack of fruit in my life, my fear that my life doesn't matter and doesn't make a difference in this world. Fill me with yourself so that in all that I do, you are evident. Leave your mark on the world through me.

9

GRACED

In these days, [the Lord] has shown his favor and
taken away my disgrace among the people.

—LUKE 1:25

Tabloid headlines trumpet news of eighty-year-old men
having babies with their twenty-three-year-old bride. So for
Zechariah, who was possibly only in his fifties, to have the
wherewithal to create a baby seems like no big deal.

For Elizabeth, this is a big deal. When they are "well along
in years," most women's wombs aren't creating a nest every
month and trying to fill it with eggs. (Although, I resent the
implication that the fifties are "well along," I realize that in
a society where people died young, fifty was much further
along the road of longevity than it would be now.) Elizabeth's
rejoicing words, "In these days, [the Lord] has shown his
favor and taken away my disgrace among the people," suggest
she certainly experienced the public's labeling of her barrenness
as disgraceful.

Disgrace is a strong word: un-graced, without the divine,
absolutely undeserved favor or assistance God offers. These
two shame-filled syllables indicate a separation from favor, a
severing of relationship. And isn't disgrace always a judgment

on someone's part? In spite of all evidence to the contrary—she had done nothing wrong—Elizabeth experienced the disgrace of barrenness, disgrace determined not by God and not by her actions, but by other people's interpretation of her situation.

This is dangerous territory, this disgracing of others. *Disgrace* is a public word—the public declaring judgment, voting its displeasure, making a decision about someone's character and God's assumed treatment of that person. The Scriptures use the word *disgrace* for Mary as well. Since her fiancé, Joseph, "did not want to expose her to public disgrace, he had in mind to divorce her quietly" (Matt. 1:19).

Grace by definition is help and favor that comes from God; so for us to declare that someone is disgraced is to assume God's role. Isn't that true anytime we cast judgment about another, for any reason whatsoever?

Because people will judge. Even good, rule-following, God-fearing people will judge. Though Luke's account makes clear that the couple's barrenness wasn't due to sin, people still secretly believed that the barrenness was God's punishment for something. "She must have sinned," they thought. "More's the pity for that priest-husband of hers. Else she'd have babies and grandbabies filling that empty nursery and her empty arms."

Some things won't change until heaven. How true is that for us today? We might never tell people to their faces, but we sure might think it: "*Tsk tsk tsk*. Bless their hearts. Well, you know how it is. You reap what you sow. Must be something going wrong for God to treat 'em like that." Or maybe we *do* tell people, straight into their broken lives, like watering the garden with battery acid, "God is surely judging you for . . ." and fill in the blank with what we assume to be a sin greater than any of ours, because, hey, look at the tragedy or void or unanswered prayer in their lives.

People— including you and me— will judge, point fingers, and whisper behind their hands. If we're not careful, we will trip over our wagging tongues and be forced to swallow all our cruel assumptions and aspersions.

Even though she didn't create a public display of her blessing, she was clear about the impact of public opinion on her. Her soft words of joy indicate how personal and painful this was: "The Lord has done this for me," she said. "In these days he has shown his favor and taken away my disgrace among the people" (Luke 1:25). In a delightful display of word play and confirmation, *favor* in the original language is *charis*.

Grace. From ungraced, to grace.

Favor is the opposite of disgrace, and God continues to flummox all our prejudices, blind judgments, and disgracing of others. Barren wombs spring to life. Priests draw near retirement and experience a dramatic renewal of faith. God tells us all day long and all our livelong lives, "See I am doing a new thing" (Isa. 43:19).

God's ability to do a new thing transcends all our limitations. And every single day, we get to watch for that new thing. May God give us eyes to peer through the darkness of our daily lives, eyes to see. Because grace is global.

And about that baby's name: The angel told Zechariah, who signed or wrote it to Elizabeth, who then nine months and eight days later told the priest and people surrounding them at the baby's circumcision, "He is to be called John."

The opposite of disgrace, the absolute absolution of any condemnation anyone could heap: *John* means "God is gracious" or "God's gracious gift."

REFLECTION

Judgment creates a dark place. When have you experienced judgment? How have you dealt with it? When have you chosen to let God sort it out so you can go on with your life of faithfulness?

How might we live, if we always delighted in God's goodness to us, God's presence in us, rather than on another's judgment of us? Talk about that gestational glow! It is neither masculine nor feminine, this filling with God and the resultant grace evident on our faces.

BENEDICTION

Dear one,
Today I delight in you,
Even though you scurry about
Like scullery mice,
Trying to grab the juiciest crumbs
And richest morsels
The world has to offer.
I know you mean well,
That you want to please others
With gifts and thoughtfulness,
Especially during this season.
But what if, today,
You revamp your wish list
And your to-do list,
And just decide
"I want to love others"?

PRAYER

Dear God, how I have cast judgment, how I have disgraced others by my words and attitudes and actions. Please forgive me. Show me how to bring favor—grace –your kindness and light, through the way I live and act in this world. For today, open my heart, hands, eyes, and life and pour out your light. Shine, Jesus. Shine through me, through all my fractured places, onto others.

10

REALLY QUIET TIME

You will be silent and not able to speak
until the day this happens.

—LUKE 1:20

What if we could witness Zechariah's wonder over the prophecy, his tenderness with his beloved wife of many years, this love of his life? What if we could see how the miracle, and the muteness, changed him?

Zechariah experienced some extended quiet time. Between Elizabeth's five-month seclusion and his inability to talk, no doubt the couple's social life diminished, as did their conversations. Zechariah was silent, and not *able* to speak even if he wanted. For a person accustomed to words, whether many or few, extended silence is torturous no matter one's personality. Even babies, who have no words, make all sorts of noises to communicate.

Silence offered Zechariah the space to listen to his own unbelief. Sometimes in silence we realize that our voices are tired, that we are weary of our own words and worries. We notice that our thoughts exhaust us and realize that we have nothing new or interesting to talk about. We tire of ourselves. In silence we wonder how people put up with our complaining and handwringing, and we see our own fear-based life in a new, quiet light.

Zechariah surely meditated with horror on his own failure and fear, reliving his question of Gabriel—"How can I know this for sure?"—and wanting to kick himself to kingdom come. But silence doesn't have to lead us to intense shame and then halt there. Silence can take us into new grace, a deep space, an internal Holy Place. There we realize that the Holy Spirit has overlaid all our wood with the gold of God's presence, the gilding of forgiveness, the fragrant aroma of heaven-scented love. There our dirge turns into praise, however silent it might sound.

There is no music I love better than Christmas hymns, unless of course it's Easter hymns, and one year I lost my voice during Advent. I couldn't sing or even hum a Christmas carol without sounding like a hybrid of an accordion and a foghorn. The voicelessness felt like such a rip-off, as though something had been stolen from me, and I went to church already barking in my soul about being shorted.

But when the music started and the first words rolled out, I sang the loudest of anyone—on the inside. All my praise welled up in a way far more meaningful than if I had been belting out notes aloud. Never has the depth of the words, the glory of the truth, felt so rich and meaningful to me. Never have I worshiped God like that, all the praise on the inside, just between me and God. The words and melody rolled around in my soul, echoing a fullness of joy and a reality of truth I'd never before experienced.

Maybe those days of gestation for Elizabeth—because Zechariah's evident lack of belief did not hinder God's deliverance on the promise of a child!—were also days of gestation for Zechariah. He had to listen deeply as the truth and glory of God, as the goodness and faithfulness of this God who delights to fulfill his promises (see Ps. 145:13), as the sheer astonishment at God's favor filled him. Maybe, there in the fields and barn, in silent prayers under bright stars and in the dark of night, alone, the words and wonder filled the belly of his soul full of God.

REFLECTION

Notice how the silence affects you day after day. Silence from God, in terms of not answering your prayers as hoped; the silence of not bearing fruit; the silence of impotence. Consider more deliberate silence on your part: stopping the flow of words to embrace the stillness and perhaps hear God's subtle voice. Is there a progression, from fidgeting to settling? What difference does silence make in your ability to listen to your soul, to God's Word, to the people in your world? How does it change you and your intersections?

BENEDICTION

Dear one,
Do you hear that,
In the midnight of your soul?
Do you hear that
Soft voice of singing,
Of wistfulness,
Of longing over you?
Because, if you will be still,
You will hear my love;
You will know that this is why I came,

To love you,
To help you love others,
With the love I pour into you.
In these quiet, still places,
I long for you to be with me,
Without your lists
And without your demands
And without any other expectation
Except that I love you,
And I always will.
Come, please,
And be still,
And let me fill
Your heart
And soul.

PRAYER

Quiet my busy mind, God, and let me find rest in the silence with you. Take away my personal agenda, the list that insists you meet my needs and fix my problems and all the demands and manipulations I bring. Fill me full of yourself, so that I can in turn give you to the world.

11

THE FIVE-MONTH RETREAT

> After this his wife Elizabeth became pregnant and for
> five months remained in seclusion. "The Lord
> has done this for me," she said.
>
> —LUKE 1:24–25

Seeing Elizabeth's joy, surprise, and gratitude must have been like witnessing the sunrise. But Zechariah's unassuming wife didn't call the reporters to get on the front page of the church newsletter. She didn't parade around in maternity clothes trying to push out her stomach to look pregnant, and she didn't write a tell-all book. She didn't run around bragging about God's superior treatment of her. I might have wanted to publicly make sure everyone knew how blessed I was, and I might even have wanted to receive some credit myself, hoping people would think, "Isn't she special? God must love her and her husband so much."

Instead, Elizabeth entirely escaped scrutiny and fame and pocketed herself away on a personal retreat. We see her centeredness as she spends five months reveling in God's faithfulness, delighting in this miracle of pregnancy, filled with God's favor and this unexpected blessing.

God heard! God knew! God answered! What a focused response on Elizabeth's part to the joyful event.

In our own lives, which render us thick-waisted with worry and wearied by work, the idea of seclusion with God seems beyond foreign. We might as well hope we win the lottery without buying tickets, it's so far-fetched. More than that, it feels like a luxury we can't possibly afford. Take time off? Time away from commitments, family, church duties, community events, Christmas pageant rehearsals? Surely this isn't the season for such extravagant self-care.

Maybe it is. Perhaps there is no better season than right now, as we experience Advent, as we look at the events leading up to Christ's birth, as we examine the character-building choices of our Advent people. When God did the most momentous miracle possible in Elizabeth's life, after a lifetime of her tending to God's presence and trying to follow the rules for relationship put down in the Torah, what did she do? She tucked herself away with this God who had answered her deepest longing.

How much more momentous is the miracle of God bringing Christ into the world and giving us life? Life we look for, long for, hope for, but cannot imagine being handed to us without our earning it. Besides, our crowded calendars taunt and nag at us with their scribbled-in boxes. How do we possibly cram yet another good thing into the days of this season without stealing time from the night? From other people who depend on us?

Maybe we make it too complicated. Five months? Not gonna happen. A day? Maybe, maybe not. OK, probably not. But remember that comfy chair at the library? Or that coffee shop that roasts its own beans, plays mellow music, and has a long, quiet lull ninety minutes before closing? What about the inn at that nearby state park, with its big rustic sofas and the hush and scent of outside sneaking in? How about a long walk in the woods or mountains or on the beach or plains near your home, with the words to Christmas carols or special Christmas Scriptures written on index cards? A few hours count as a personal retreat—wherever we can hide out with the One who came for us becomes a getaway possibility.

Elizabeth's seclusion ended with Mary's visit. Is it possible that Elizabeth's sensitivity to Mary, her exuberant welcome of the girl, and her recognition of the child she carried, were made possible by her intense time of joyful celebration alone with God?

That brand of welcome comes from time in God's light. What if we soaked up so much Son, if we were so saturated, that all the Christmas jostling would make Jesus spill out in brilliance? That would be so appealing to the people sitting in this world's darkness, it would fly right on the top of their wish list.

REFLECTION

When have you experienced some concentrated personal retreat time with God? What did you like or not like about the time? And how could you create some space to tuck away this season? Where might you go?

BENEDICTION

Dear one,
What joy, what privilege,
To know that you draw near to me,

Not because I give good gifts,
But because you want to be together so much
That you set aside time
To devote to our relationship
In little ways and in big ways,
And always
Trying to find a way for us.
I promise that when you draw near to me
I will draw near to you.
Try it, just try it,
And see.

PRAYER

This all sounds good, Lord. But my calendar, my life, my commitments . . . my excuses, God. Forgive me for allowing — and putting   so much in the calendar and forgetting you, for getting to plan time with you beyond a hurried "good morning" or "thank you for this day." You are the best part of my day and of this season. Help me to retreat with you.

12

MOST FAVORED STATUS?

Greetings, you who are highly favored!
The Lord is with you.

—LUKE 1:28

She was just a child, perhaps thirteen or fourteen, and engaged to be married. Mary likely filled her days helping at home, filling her hope chest, and filling her mind with dreams of marriage to this man named Joseph, who was busy preparing a room for them to live in. He would return at a surprise date, and the wedding procession would begin with a trumpet sound. She needed to be ready, so her bridegroom didn't catch her unprepared.

So when the teenager looked up from her innocent, young life and heard the greeting of an angel, saw a form and face such as few in history had ever witnessed, what did she think? His opening salutation, "Greetings, you who are highly favored! The Lord is with you," perplexed her, given that she was young, poor, unmarried, and uneducated.

When heaven shows up at your doorstep, calls you highly favored, and reminds you that the Lord is with you . . . alarm, dread, and total uncertainty must wrinkle your brow.

The word here for favored is *graced*, which is nice enough, and then the angel modified that with the word *highly*. This evidently did not set Mary's mind at ease, because Luke tell us that "Mary was greatly troubled at his words and wondered what kind of greeting that might be." His opening line was not a typical address for the likes of her. Her social status might have read, "Insignificant girl and her insignificant life in an insignificant town."

Mary's highly favored status took her to the gracious arms of her relative Elizabeth, whose hospitality was an enormous grace, because the world would look with terrible grimness on Mary's pregnancy. Even Mary's betrothed, Joseph, was going to divorce her quietly so as not to make a public show of her supposed unfaithfulness.

Highly favored? When we deem others highly favored, we mean that doors have opened to fame or fortune for them. The favored horse in a race is the one that's supposed to win. Favor means good things happen. People like you, make a way for you. This wasn't the case with the young woman visited by an angel.

Look at what happened to Mary after the angel Gabriel's proclamation. Favor is not for the faint of heart.

The route of favor for Mary wasn't a first-class pass on a luxury liner or an A-lister's tour. It took her through public scorn, the closed doors and full quarters of innkeepers or relatives when she was in the pangs of childbirth, a stable for a birthing room, and then exile to Egypt when the tiny family ran for their lives. In spite of the blessings she treasured along the way, like Anna and Simeon at Jesus' circumcision (see Luke 2:25–39), Mary stored up far more than kind words.

The journey of favor forced her to watch helplessly as crowds mocked, spat, and discredited her grown son. To witness the maniacal downward spiral of jealous leaders and the shrugging passivity of others. To watch betrayal with a fist clamped at her heart. To overhear verbal jousts challenging Christ. To see a crown of thorns shoved over her adult child's battered head, spikes driven into his wrists, and him raised up onto an instrument of torture and shame—the cross. To dress his limp, lifeless body with temporary burial ointments, to cradle him one last time. This man, whom she had cradled in her arms and sung lullabies over, running her mother-fingers over his tiny face and kissing his soft baby cheeks, she would cradle his bloodied face one last time on the journey to the tomb.

We can't have Christmas without a cross on the horizon, not really. Because Christ's coming is rendered irrelevant if we understand it to mean that we can hitch a ride to easy street, that everyone will love us, and that we will always get the job, the raise, the trophy spouse, and all the blessings and riches in the world's definition of favor.

Maybe this is one reason why the angel's answers to her question, "How will this be, since I am a virgin?" (Luke 1:34) included the declaration, "For nothing will be impossible with God" (Luke 1:37 NASB). This is not to be confused with the "falsism," "God only gives you want you can handle." I think God regularly allows in our lives far more than we can handle so that we are forced to turn and rely on the One with whom "nothing will be impossible." Mary might have agreed.

Because in spite of all the unknowns, all the risks involved, everything that she might lose, Mary affirmed the angel's proclamation with, "I am the Lord's servant. May your word to me be fulfilled" (Luke 1:38).

REFLECTION

Where have you experienced favor from others? What do you think favor from God should look like? How's that idea working for you? When have you been able to say, "I am the Lord's servant. May it be to me as you have said"?

BENEDICTION

Dear one,
No rose gardens were promised,
Unless you count the flowers
In the garden of the tomb.
But here is my promise to you:
Nothing is impossible with me.
And if you grip my hand,
We will see incredible adventures
And also great pain.
And I promise you this as well:
I will give you far more than you can handle
But not more than I can handle.
And I will be with you
The entire route
All the way to resurrection.

PRAYER

God, I want to say yes, like Mary, to whatever "favor" means in your plans, hopes, and dreams for my life. Nothing is impossible with you. I will hold on to you, knowing that with me, much of life is impossible. But not with you. Help me to say, "May it be to me as you have said."

13

MARY'S RESPONSE

I am the Lord's servant. . . .
May your word to me be fulfilled.

—LUKE 1:38

After Gabriel's announcement, in spite of all the questions spilling into her mind, Mary's sole recorded words in response were, "How will this be, since I am a virgin?"

Didn't Zechariah ask a similar question, and was struck speechless, his lips sealed until the proof of the prophecy was born? He incurred quite a penalty for his doubt there in the Holy Place with an angel towering over him.

Gabriel first sought out Zechariah, who was supposedly mature of both form and faith, with years of priestly service, and he asked, "How can I be sure of this?" Next on the angel's visitation list came Mary, who wondered, not how she could be sure, but almost out of curiosity, "How will this happen? I don't get it." Maybe she knew some version of the facts of life, and Joseph sure didn't seem to be included in the angel's proclamation.

The angel started his overwhelming answer with, "The Holy Spirit will come on you, and the power of the Most High will overshadow you" (Luke 1:35 NASB). A Jewish woman might be familiar with the concept of overshadowing, if she knew any of the Israelites' history, because this was how they referred to God's presence when it hovered over the people, the tabernacle, and the Holy of Holies. The presence, the power of the mighty God, the Most High God, the only God, encamped over the Israelites' tabernacle during their desert journey to the Promised Land. Later God's presence overshadowed all the elements of the Most Holy Place and filled it with luminous glory.

Overshadow. I want this. I want God to overshadow me. This idea of hovering and covering by God, that God's work might be born in me, born through me . . . this is what I want for Christmas, and for every single day of my life. When someone is overshadowed by another being or object, the otherness takes center stage. Whether we're overshadowed literally by a giant oak tree or overshadowed figuratively by someone else's more intriguing presence, we diminish in stature and importance as well as in power.

God overshadows no matter what, because the Most High God is, well, most high. There is none other, and my internal posture or external posturing changes nothing about God. But I want to acquiesce to that, to partner with that; I want to don Mary's humility, the attitude of heart that says, "Yes, cover me so that others see not me but you."

But the angel wasn't finished and next delivered a mind-spinning sentence: "So the holy one to be born will be called the Son of God" (Luke 1:35). Did this circle around like an antiphon in Mary's mind—"the Son of God, the Son of God, holy one, holy one"? Because, weren't these the words people had been awaiting for hundreds of years? The Holy One, the Son of God, the long-awaited Messiah, *that* one? And this insignificant woman in her insignificant life in her insignificant village surely held her breath, her eyes wide and her heart thumping.

Thankfully, Gabriel didn't leave her hanging there, twirling in the breeze of wonder, her mind tangled with "Pinch me, I can't believe this is happening," "Did I just imagine that?" and "What does this mean, really, long term?" The angel wrapped up his birth announcement with the gift of community and family: "Even Elizabeth your relative is going to have a child in her old age, and she who was said to be unable to conceive is in her sixth month" (Luke 1:36).

Sixth month? God had been pushing aside the curtain of silence for six months already, and Elizabeth also was having a baby? Dramatic and amazing things were happening in her kin's life as well—how comforting to Mary. What a kind and beautiful way for the angel to deal with Mary's question and fear, reassuring her of companionship. She would not be alone during this time.

And finally, the absolute blessing of the angel's final words: "For nothing will be impossible with God." Nothing, nothing, nothing.

Old barren women, innocent teenage girls, priests, fiancés, fidgeting people, and a world draped in blackout curtains shrouded in disappointment, disbelief, and flat-out discouragement. Nothing is impossible with God.

The dark became light, barrenness became blessing, and a babe would be born who would change the world forever.

May we enter into that impossibility with Mary.

Though the angel left her, God never did. May we, too, be so overshadowed by God's presence that, no matter what, we embrace the day's impossibilities—indeed, life's impossibilities—with God's possibility.

REFLECTION

Where do you want to be overshadowed, *need* to be overshadowed? When have you experienced that? What is your greatest impossibility right now? How can you instead focus on God's ability, God's promise?

BENEDICTION

Dear one,
Let the words
Ring in your soul.
Nothing,
Nothing,
Nothing,
Is impossible with me.
Your greatest doubts,
Your largest fears,
Your smallest concerns,
Your tiniest perplexities.
Nothing is impossible
With me.
Go ahead—make your list
And then watch for my hand.
Come under my shelter;
Let me cover you
With my protection
And presence.
From that place

It is simple to say,
"Be it done to me . . ."

PRAYER

God, help me to trust your covering, to not be afraid of anyone's shadow including my own, but rather to let you overshadow me with your will, your plans, your love. Help me to rest in that safety.

14

NO MORE LET SIN

You are to give him the name Jesus,
because he will save his people from their sins.

—MATTHEW 1:21

That night began in the usual way. Go to bed exhausted, plan to sleep deeply, wake up refreshed, and start all over again. But this night was different. Joseph was beyond exhausted. Worry dogged every step and dug premature furrows on his forehead. His fiancé had shown up and claimed to be pregnant with a fantastic, unbelievable story about an angel, God, and her carrying God's child. She'd been so stable, he thought as he tossed on his pallet. She'd seemed like a perfect match-up to their parents' ways of thinking. But now this? Joseph had figured he would come to love her eventually, like couples in most arranged marriages, though that wasn't essential. But not now, not with this development. Was she really hiding her unfaithfulness from him and trying to blame it on God?

His head pounded, and he rolled over yet again. The only possibility, he thought, was to just divorce her. A hush-hush divorce. He shook his head in the dark and clenched his teeth until his jaws ached. That wouldn't shut the mouths of the gossips, not at all. They would chew over this morsel for months, until the next victim appeared. He felt bad for the girl and her baby, too, for Mary really was barely past childhood. So young. But what else could he do? He couldn't salvage her reputation, but at least he could try to dull the roar of village voices.

At last he slipped into a restless sleep, and an angel slipped into his slumber. "Marry Mary, Joseph. She's telling you the truth. Her son—indeed, God's Son—will be born, and 'you are to give him the name Jesus, because he will save his people from their sins'" (Matt. 1:20–21).

"Save his people from their sins"? Who talked like that, anyway? It wasn't anything he heard at temple on the Sabbath. The priests might not have a job, if they didn't need to enforce all the laws of the Torah. *Saved* from sin? This entirely broke with the Pharisees' traditions and rules.

Saving people from sins just wasn't best-selling stuff. It still isn't. But sin was, and has always been, the ball-and-chain we drag around with us, never able to hack off the thick links and shake ourselves free. The shackles rub sores on our skin, deep gashes of regret and disappointment in ourselves and others. Then they cut clear through to the bone, and still we are powerless to saw through them. And no one has a key. Sin is the ugliness no one wants to mention, the scar on our souls that causes people to politely avert their gaze or avoid us altogether.

And meantime, this brokenness ruptures all our relationships. Relationships between us and others, us and God. Between us and ourselves, too, to slice it personally, because when we rupture, we separate ourselves from the people God created us to be. Isaiah warned us of this; "Your iniquities have separated you from your God; your sins have hidden his face from you, so that he will not hear" (Isa. 59:2). And here, I too want to turn away, to avert my gaze, because isn't this the truth for us all? We are powerless to change this core essence. Powerless.

But thanks be to God. "He was appalled that there was no one to intervene; so his own arm worked salvation for him, and his own righteousness sustained him" (Isa. 59:16).

What did the angel say? "He will save his people from their sins."

Save . . .

His people . . .

From their sins.

God's own arm working out salvation, doing what we cannot. How much better can the news be? If that's not best-selling, nothing is. The answer to the question, "Why did Christ come to earth?" isn't, "So we could go to heaven." It isn't, "To keep us out of hell," nor, "So we could be forgiven." It's all that, of course, but the root reason? The essence of Christ's coming is to save us from our sins—to set us free.

And since that's the truth, I want to start living like someone who has been saved from her sins. Isaac Watts's great Christmas carol rings out, "No more let sins and sorrows grow."[1] I can't let sin grow any longer, because sin is the opposite of Advent, of Christ's coming.

When Joseph awakened, the dream still imprinted on his soul, he knew what to do. To judge Mary and divorce her would rupture his reputation, though not so deeply as it would harm Mary. He had to take her as his wife. He would honor this coming. Because the child she carried would save Joseph from *his* own sin.

Joseph shook his head. "Jesus," they would call him. He didn't understand it. But as he slipped on his sandals, he couldn't stop smiling, and he ran all the way to Mary's house. Freedom, it turned out, was right around the corner.

REFLECTION

In what ways is sin a forbidden topic of conversation? How do you react to someone pointing out your sin? (It's hard to be grateful for someone else's honesty, isn't it?) When are you most vulnerable to sin? When have you allowed sin to rupture a relationship?

BENEDICTION

Dear one,
It's still the best news ever and always—
Sending my Son
To deliver you
From your sins.
Isn't that what you're really hoping for?
To be set free
From the shackles of sin
That leads to shame
And traps you
Again and again?
And just think!
The sunrise would
Rise all day long
When my people
Turn to me

And get set free.
Otherwise how will people know?
How will you grow?
Turn to me,
Get set free,
And the world will say,
"Don't they look just like Jesus?"
Advent
Every day
Through you.

PRAYER

Lord, I confess I rupture relationships so often. Please forgive me and set me free. No more let sin and sorrow grow in me. Rather, let Christ come day after day through the way I live.

NOTE

1. Isaac Watts, "Joy to the World," 1719, *The United Methodist Hymnal* (Nashville: Cokesbury, 1989), 246.

WEEK 3 OF ADVENT

15

LEAPING JOY

The Third Sunday of Advent

As soon as the sound of your greeting reached my ears,
the baby in my womb leaped for joy.

—LUKE 1:44

The angel's words sang in Mary's mind, accompanying and reassuring her all the way to the Judean hill country where she would see Elizabeth. She was with child! She would give birth to a son! They would call him Jesus! It was huge and overwhelming. It was terrifying and wonderful.

Elizabeth dragged open the door and pulled Mary into the room. Imagine their embrace, young Mary leaning over Elizabeth's six-months-pregnant tummy to wrap her youthful arms around Elizabeth.

At the sound of Mary's voice, the baby leaped in Elizabeth's womb. Did Mary feel him thump against her own still-taut tummy? The baby who would be called John responded to the voice of the mother of his Lord. This single revelation should be enough to carry everyone through the rest of their lives.

But God wasn't through with the reassurances, and in fact, is never finished reassuring us. Throughout our lives, there will be leaping moments when we are absolutely certain that

God has spoken, that God is present, that God is guiding, and we will make it through.

"As soon as the sound of your greeting reached my ears, the baby in my womb leaped for joy," Elizabeth marveled (Luke 1:44).

The baby didn't just leap. The baby leaped *for joy*.

Oh, joy of all joys. The joy of their salvation was in the room with them, the unborn John dancing in delight. What a gift of confirmation and wonder for both women.

Maybe Elizabeth remembered the angel's words to her husband about their yet-to-be conceived son: "He will be a joy and delight to you, and many will rejoice because of his birth" (Luke 1:14). There was a whole lot of joy happening, joy that eclipsed the darkness of the times, the fear of both the known and the unknown. And John who would bring joy, leaped for joy over the One who would come and surpass him.

Jumping for joy: such a beautiful picture of this quickening, and the supernatural events occurring in their midst. And John, the first responder to the Christ!

Years later, John's followers were anxious about people shifting allegiances and turning toward Jesus (see John 3:28–31). John addressed their concerns. He said, "The friend who attends the bridegroom waits and listens for him and is full of joy when he hears the bridegroom's voice" (v. 29). Throughout his adult ministry, John waited, listened, and was full of joy when he heard the Bridegroom's voice.

I want to learn to watch and wait and listen for the Bridegroom's voice everywhere I go, looking to find him around me, to proclaim him. To leap in testimony of who Jesus is. How I would love for my soul to leap every time I saw another human being. To leap with recognition that that person bears God's image and that every single person is loved by God. How this would change the way I intersect with every single person, in every single place and life circumstance. The homeless man selling newspapers, trying to earn an honest living—I am going to buy that paper from him the next time I see him. And the woman cleaning the restroom at the airport—I'm going to tell her what a beautiful smile she has, what a great job she does, and that I hope she finds favor with her employer.

I'm going to leap for joy by over-tipping the underpaid people at the coffee shop. The employees at the Everything's-a-Buck store, the bus driver, and the child who stomped on my feet crawling to his seat—I'm going to greet them with the joy of recognition that this is one Jesus was born to save. And when I'm with others in ministry, I'm going to leap for joy at God's work through them, just as John did when the Lamb of God appeared (see John 1:29–36).

For are these not all known by God? Aren't they stamped with a brand that says, "Made by God"? And don't they carry the same blessing as I do—"Before you were born, I knew you" (see Jer. 1:5)? Don't they deserve a sign from us that the Savior has come, some evidence of the joy of the Savior like John gave?

Wouldn't we all be leaping about like gazelles at this amazing good news: God has come to us in Christ; God has come to free us from our sin; God has made salvation plain in this world through the Son?

Joy, joy, joy. Joy given, joy restored, salvation en route. Maybe it's time to get this party started.

REFLECTION

Where have you "leaped for joy" like John? How often do you experience joy? What is your soul response to others? Is it situational or consistent?

BENEDICTION

Dear one,
How I long
To see that joy
Leap into your eyes
And leap into your actions
And leap from your very soul.
Because I love you
And I have formed you
And I rejoiced
At your birth,
Just like many
Rejoiced at John's.
You are no less
A miracle;
And I want you to know,
And to live in,
The joy
Of my salvation,
My sending my salvation
To you,
For you,
For the world.
So leap for joy,
And watch where you land,
And love well.

PRAYER

How I want my joy-response to overflow spontaneously. I want to recognize the presence of Christ in everyone, everyone who bears the stamp and image of God. Everyone. Help me, God. Help me to start with your joy in me and your image in me—wonder of wonders—and help me then to show genuine joy to everyone I meet.

16

SHARING THE LIGHT

At that time, Mary got ready and hurried to the hill country of Judea, where she entered Zechariah's home and greeted Elizabeth.

—LUKE 1:39–40

How vulnerable Mary must have felt, knowing that she carried within her the One promised to King David so long ago. What a lot of responsibility, knowing that, "The holy one to be born will be called the Son of God," as Gabriel said (Luke 1:35). This young girl likely wanted nothing more than to be with someone who would understand, someone further along the road of pregnancy and life than she was. Someone to explain the mysterious changes in her body. No way she wanted to be alone with this news, this good but scary news, and this bewildering place of favor. But also, Mary surely knew of Elizabeth's devotion to God, of her spiritual maturity and righteousness. All the more reason for Mary to hurry to her kin's home.

No one should be alone in surprising, difficult, or even glorious times—because these are all more manageable when shared with another. But they are more than manageable. When we have companions on the journey, we somehow intersect with God and our own souls better. Colors are brighter, beauty more beautiful, funny things funnier when shared. In community, courage increases and fear decreases.

Besides, God created us for community, and it was no accident that Elizabeth, formerly barren, was great with child and could help Mary with all the messiness of the first trimester of pregnancy. The angel Gabriel's words offered both encouragement ("You aren't alone in this surprising place; Elizabeth is expecting, too") and instruction ("Head there right away, so you won't be alone, and in that place, all this will be confirmed to you").

Mary headed right over, like the angel ordered, because she needed to be in a judgment-free zone, a place where no one condemned her and someone guided her forward, deliberately and generously.

Mary knew about Elizabeth's pregnancy. But Elizabeth knew nothing about the child Mary carried. The older woman's attentiveness to the Holy Spirit had been honed in the months since conception, as she'd sung, prayed, rested, and worked about her home. She'd tuned out others' voices, and even her husband, bless his heart, couldn't talk just then.

In all that quiet serenity, Elizabeth listened. She knew only that the child she herself carried would prepare the way for the Anointed One, the Messiah, the One they'd all been waiting for. She had no idea who would bring him into the world . . . until Mary appeared at the door.

Sensitive after her quiet months, she recognized God's presence coming down the path. Right there at the door, Elizabeth identified the holy glow. The Holy Spirit filled Elizabeth, and she burst out with a blessing that must have soothed and encouraged Mary every day for the rest of her life: "Blessed are you among women, and blessed is the child you will bear! But why am I so favored that the mother of my Lord should come to me?" (Luke 1:42–43).

Favored. Graced. Gifted. Again and again and again, Elizabeth was graced. Isn't this so, for us as well? Graced by the presence of our Lord and Savior, who appears to us regularly through the Scriptures, through the lives and actions of people we know, and through the miraculous and the mundane of our lives. Graced by his life within us, his Holy Spirit sealing us. Graced lives. Like Mary's.

Elizabeth demonstrated that grace by accepting Mary and by her exuberant proclamation. Mentors have the courage to speak aloud what God whispers within them. Elizabeth didn't mumble this under her breath as though uncertain of what she said. She didn't use her inside voice. She exclaimed in a loud voice. Loud and clear she proclaimed what she knew to be true: "Blessed are you! Blessed is the child you will bear!" (see Luke 1:42).

A mentor is simply further along the road of life and experience with God than we are and is willing to share that insight with us. For the rest of Elizabeth's pregnancy, and likely right through John's birth, she mentored Mary, tutoring her in listening to God, in managing pregnancy, and in being a homemaker. And don't mentors help us recognize those moments where our faith must leap, those places that cannot be explained away as coincidence? We forget when the way gets dark, the path rutted and covered over with low-hanging vines. At night, it's hard to remember to walk by the previous day's light.

When Zechariah returned home from the fields that first night and wiped his feet on the doormat, he hardly knew what to do with himself. The door swung open, and light poured out. His house, his mature, quiet house with his mature, serene wife, now filled with happy teenage chatter and deep conversations, good smells from the cooking fire, and the warmth of love.

Hard to know who was more blessed.

I imagine Zechariah, sitting in his easy chair after dinner, watching the goings-on of the two pregnant women — one the love of his life carrying the child of his dreams, and the other the mother of his Lord. Life just couldn't get any better than this. And his weathered face broke into a smile, his eyes nearly squeezed shut. His silent laughter shook his shoulders, and he laughed until tears slipped down his cheeks.

Joy and gladness. Yes sir. Joy and gladness.

REFLECTION
Who has offered you a judgment-free zone? To whom have you offered the same? What people have mentored you, and how have you grown from that relationship?

BENEDICTION
Dear one,
Joy and gladness
Multiply when shared,
And fear shrinks.
It is not good to be alone
In the good times
Or the hard times,

The unexpected times
Or the expectedly hard times.
Come to me.
This is a judgment-free zone.
And together we will find a way through
The good and the bad,
The happy and the sad,
Joy and gladness.
Joy and gladness.

PRAYER

Some alone time is good, Lord, but when I'm alone too much, I know I miss out. Help me to reach out into others' lives and share some of the light you've given me, and help me to find others who will shine a light on my path.

17

REMEMBERING MERCY

His mercy extends to those who fear him,
from generation to generation.

—LUKE 1:50

Mercy showed up at Mary's door one sparkling day, and Mary ran right to her relative's home with the good news. The bubbling stream of Mary's song finally overflowed its banks. Right there in the house of the man named "God Remembers," her theme of rescue, of God's mercy, rang through her lyrics in full and practical display. Five times the word *mercy* appears in Luke's first chapter, a resonant choral round of God's bright breaking-in through the darkness.

Mercy breaking through! Mercy, the absolute antithesis of people's experience, both in the first century and even now— people trapped in systems of oppression, in economic or physical distress, in damaging or damaged relationships with not a shred of hope for change. And then mercy, extended from heaven like sunrise—feeding the hungry! Scattering enemies! Bringing down rulers! Mercy, the difference between midnight and high noon.

How good that Mary turned it into song, because then she and the people with her and after her would remember it for generations to come. Music hides itself in parts of our soul inaccessible in other ways, returning to our consciousness in vital and timely manners. Mary would need to remember, as she pressed her way through the hills, dells, and dark shadows of her life. This young woman—whose name actually means "song"—would need to remember that God remembered to be merciful and that mercy wins in the long run, in spite of the shorter, terrifying run she'd experience in the next days and years. Because she would be on the run—she and Joseph and their brand-new baby, running from Herod off to Egypt, then running to hide out in an obscure village called Nazareth from Herod's wicked son, the next generation of tainted monarchy.

And don't we need to remember, too? We run constantly into, through, around, and because of darkness. Remember that God in Christ remembered, showing us compassion, a deep and active movement of kindness to us in our despair and doubt. We remember our dire situations and that mercy is an active word, a reaching out to those in serious need.

Mercy shows up at our door, too, just like it did for Mary. "For the mighty one has done great things for me," Mary sang. And then she sang of God's incredible acts of mercy and displays of remembrance through Christ.

So we, too, remember. What mighty things has God done for us? Make a list, write it down, sing it over and over, and God's mercy in Christ becomes our mercy through Christ. That mercy flows into the world, then through our actions. Every time we wipe another's tears or open our homes, hearts, or wallets; every time we fill a sandbag, change a diaper, offer bread to the hungry, or lend a hand to the feeble; every time we visit the prisoner, mow the neighbor's lawn, or shovel someone's snow, God demonstrates mercy through us. And the miraculous gift of mercy extends from generation to generation, from the beginning of time to the tips of our very fingers and the tip of our tongue.

We live, we speak, we act, we love with mercy, always aware that our very brokenness is mended in Christ's coming, and so we, too, with our hands and hearts, can stitch together others' brokenness with the threads of Christ's mercy.

God has "helped his servant Israel, remembering to be merciful" (Luke 1:54). And now we are Israel, grafted into that tree, and God remembers, and we remember deep in our soul's DNA. Mercy lives on through us, one lifelong extension of compassion and kindness. God reaches out in Christ, and Christ through us, and the world becomes a kinder, more compassionate place. A merciful place. All because God remembered, Mary said yes, and God's song lives on and never ends until the kingdom comes.

And we say? Christ, have mercy.

And he does, because he is mercy. He does mercy. He has mercy. Toward us, through us. We remember, with Mary: mercy wins.

REFLECTION

When has mercy appeared at your door? Who wears the face of mercy for you? When have you received mercy? Offered mercy? Where do you need mercy? Need to remember God's mercy? Need to offer mercy?

BENEDICTION

Dear one,
I remembered.
I have not forgotten
My promise of mercy
To you and yours
And to all who came
Before you
And to all who follow
From generation to generation.
I extend mercy,
Kind acts of compassion
Through my Son
And through my people
And through the world
I fashioned for you.
Please remember
That as you have so
Freely received,
Freely give
Mercy upon mercy
From the rising of the sun
To the rising of the moon
And all the moments in-between.
Mercy scatters darkness
Just like the sun,
Just like my Son.
So scatter away.

PRAYER

I do forget, God—in all my fear, I forget mercy. Mercy you've given me and mercy from others. Your tender mercies from on high never end—may they continue through me into this dark world. I say with all the company of saints, Christ have mercy.

18

ZECHARIAH'S SONG

Because of the tender mercy of our God, by which
the rising sun will come to us from heaven, to shine on
those living in darkness and in the shadow of death,
to guide our feet into the path of peace.

—LUKE 1:78–79

Eight days after the birth of their long-awaited baby, eight long days filled with mute wonder and joy.... Seriously, wasn't Zechariah ricocheting off the walls out of a crazy delight in his wife, their son, and God's amazing work, this miracle of birth to a couple perhaps thirty or more years childless? For eight days, Zechariah and Elizabeth prepared for John's circumcision. In that world, the eighth day was the traditional day of naming, and the traditional way was to name the child after the grandfather or father.

After gathering at the priest's home, the people began to address the child as "Zechariah, son of Mr. God Remembers," because didn't God, after all, remember? Elizabeth stopped them, her silent husband still unable to speak because he hadn't believed the angel Gabriel. Elizabeth said, "No! He is to be called John" (Luke 1:60).

They protested. "No one in your whole family tree is called John." I don't think they pressed because she was a woman and therefore her thoughts were irrelevant. Rather, I think, because John was such a foreign name to them. They probably didn't even know anyone named John. It caused quite a hullabaloo, to call this newborn anything except the son of God Remembers.

And then the father entered the fray. He grabbed a wooden tablet coated with wax and scrawled, "His name is John." Immediately his tongue loosened, and his praise poured out. God had not forgotten his people. God had raised up a horn, set out a megaphone in the voice of the one who would call from the wilderness, years later. God remembered and was showing mercy to them all.

After all those months of silence, of meditating on God's work, God's provision, and his own lack of faith, after finding mercy and joy in the quiet center of his soul, when Zechariah spoke, his words rolled out in well-rounded praise, a soliloquy of joy and prophecy. In his forced muteness, Zechariah had encountered God's glory and embraced the miracle of God's purpose and provision. His name will be John — grace, God is gracious, God's gracious gift.

The father's words at the circumcision and naming of his son redirect us to God, to God's amazing grace. From the disgrace of barrenness to the gracious gift of a son called "God Is Gracious."

Zechariah and Elizabeth are not mentioned after John's circumcision. We see their lives for only nine or ten months, and then they disappear from the pages of Scripture. Yet what an impact. From them we learn the power of faithfulness, the essentialness of not losing hope and of continuing to pray. Of trusting that God has not forgotten and of remembering that

God's promises are certain. Through them we meet grace and witness wisdom and hospitality. They have attended to God, listened, grown, received forgiveness, welcomed others, been embraced by grace and favor, and recognized the Christ child in a pregnant teen.

Even as their son prepared the way for the Messiah, so they prepare the way for us to follow God.

Their faith and presence are critical to our own journeys, not just because they gave birth to and parented the one who would blaze the trail for the Anointed One, but also because they show us how to wait, hold fast, pray, praise, and keep showing up to daily life, in spite of disappointment and unanswered prayer.

And what happens? People, in response, are filled with wonder. They rejoice. They recognize that God is up to more than they could possibly imagine or hope for. So it was during the birth of John. (See Luke 1:59–66.)

May it be so for us as well. Because of our *yes*, may people know God's tender mercies—the light that delivers from darkness and the shadow of death and illuminates the path of peace.

REFLECTION

Where have you seen God's amazing, gracious answer? And, when have people celebrated with you, declaring truly that God is gracious because of God's work in your life? When haven't they celebrated?

BENEDICTION

Dear one,
I am gracious.
I am God
Who is gracious.
And that grace extends
To you and to your loved ones
And becomes a light
On the dark path.
Carry the light,
Give grace to others,
The gift they truly crave
In a world without grace
Locked into the darkness
Of longings unfulfilled
And dreams undreamed.
And find others to hike with you
On that path;
Find people who live faithfulness
And continue to trust
Even in the dark.

PRAYER

God, help me to dwell well in this dark world, to trust you, to look for your gracious gifts, and to become grace to others. For then the light will fall on the right pathways and lead us all to peace.

19

THE BRANCH ON JOSEPH'S TREE

She will give birth to a son, and you are to
give him the name Jesus.

—MATTHEW 1:21

While we know Mary stayed with Elizabeth for three months, we don't have any idea where Joseph had taken himself. If he was like most other bridegrooms, he was measuring and sawing and hammering at his parents' house as he built a room for his new bride, so that they had a place to live once they married.

Joseph descended from the line of David, and when he looked back over his adventurous ancestors, no doubt he wiped his brow and hoped for a nice, quiet life with his nice, sweet wife in a nice, little place. And his kinfolk weren't skeletons hidden away in the closet; no, their antics were noted in Israel's records and Scriptures. However much of a heroine in Israel's history she was, Joseph's great-great-great-great grandmother Rahab was a prostitute, liar, traitor, and Gentile from the city of Jericho.

Then her grandson, King David, spied a woman named Bathsheba bathing, let out a wolf whistle, and wanted her for his wife, so he brought her to his palace, and she conceived.

Whoops, one thing—she was already married. No problem. He was the king. He could overrule that detail. He arranged to have her husband removed from the picture by forcing the troops to withdraw from him in battle, thus letting the highly respected military man be murdered. God was not pleased— to say the least. King David married Bathsheba, but the new- lywed couple's first child died. However, the second one was told he would sit on the throne and that from him the Anointed One would be born. Fortunately, God kept track of which of King Solomon's many wives would birth the next generation that would bring the world that much closer to the promised Messiah, the forever heir to the throne.

But before too long, a king had a son who was so evil that he filled the streets of Jerusalem with innocent blood (see 2 Kings 21:16). Thankfully King Manasseh repented and the family line continued (see 2 Chron. 33:10–20). And in spite of all the bloodshed and bad blood of God's chosen people, God kept reaching out, forgiving, and keeping promises. More babies were born, generation after generation of them, all forming a long line of David's progeny.

And then, out of the thick darkness, light pierced their long night of the soul and reached into the lives of an engaged couple in a small town called Nazareth. When Joseph learned of Mary's pregnancy, he stopped hammering and sawing and opted for a quiet divorce, although how that was possible in a small village I don't know. Even if he fol- lowed "private" protocol and issued her a writ of divorce in the presence of two witnesses, word would still travel. And Mary would still be pregnant and thus shamed by society. If her parents refused to take her in, or if they died, then she and the child would surely be destitute.

But Joseph was a righteous man, faithful to God's law, Matthew tells us, and Joseph wanted no harm to come to this young woman. He just didn't know what to think about her morals. He probably wanted to believe her, but then again, what a fantastic story to swallow, like choking down a whale. Mary's story of a divine pregnancy was the stuff of pagan mythology. Divorce seemed the only tenable option to Joseph.

And then an angel interrupted his sleep, telling him, "Joseph son of David, do not be afraid to take Mary home as your wife, because what is conceived in her is from the Holy Spirit" (Matt. 1:20).

The angel called Joseph's lineage to his mind: "Remember, you came from King David, so this will all come together. 'The child is mine,' God said. You will raise him as your own, he will be your son and will fit into your family tree just fine, and you will call him Jesus, the Christ, the Anointed One, the Messiah. Because he will save his people from their sins."

Joseph woke up, shook the sleep from his eyes, and headed off to find Mary and bring her home with him.

How's that for obedience?

Maybe it's easier to obey when an angel enters your dreams. But Joseph was in the habit of obedience. He was a righteous man, sensitive to the Holy Spirit's promptings and to the people around him. Maybe he recognized the angel's words and related them to Isaiah's prophecy: "The virgin will conceive and give birth to a son, and will call him Immanuel"—which means "God with us" (see Isa. 7:14).

And as surely as God had been with all the people in the past, so God would be with all the people to come. May God give us, like Joseph, ears to hear, eyes to recognize, and the heart to follow.

REFLECTION

When have you seen righteousness become self-righteousness and harm others? In whom do you see this? Yourself? Someone you love? How does this impact you? And how can you listen and follow, love and protect like Joseph?

BENEDICTION

Dear one,
No matter your lineage,
You are now grafted into my tree.
Because Immanuel,
God with you,
Is with you,
You are not alone,
And you are part of this royal line
The skeletons in your closet
Can't harm you,
And in fact glorify me all the more
Because of my work
In you
And through you.
So sleep deeply,
Listen for kindness,
And love well
When you awaken,
Because the world needs
The love we offer.

PRAYER

God, I look backward and am embarrassed. I look inward and am ashamed. Clear me of my guilt and awaken me from dormancy, awaken your righteousness within me. Please show me what it will look like, for you to provide for me, and to protect and love me, and then through me.

20

THE TIME CAME

While they were there, the time came for the baby to
be born, and she gave birth to her firstborn, a son.

—LUKE 2:6–7

The streets were crowded, the houses jammed, and the
inns overflowing with people in the little town. Bethlehem
rejoiced under the influx of visitors, and the vendors tallied
receipts with glee. Joseph and Mary arrived in the City of
David to register, along with all the other cousins, aunts, and
uncles in the entire line of David, waiting in lines and hoping
for accommodations. Relatives chattered and reintroduced
themselves. Adults patted children's heads and said, "My,
how you've grown. I'd never have recognized you."

Into this melee, after a ninety-mile hike, Joseph stood
on tiptoe and peered around unknown kinfolk, hoping to
recognize someone, anyone, desperate to find a spot for his
betrothed to rest. Nine months pregnant and a journey like
that! No wonder Mary looked like labor could begin any
moment. With precious little time to waste, Joseph did more
than glance around. He knocked and then pounded on every
door he could find. And people wanted to help, no doubt they
did. But that government-ordered census filled every single

berth and bed full of people; every square foot of space jammed. People, people everywhere, and not a room to rent.

At door after door, nephews and cousins, aunts and uncles and great-great relatives shook their heads sadly. There literally wasn't any room for this twosome about to become three. The couple turned to leave, and it was hard to know if they or their hopes were more exhausted.

"But, wait," someone said, eying them with pity. "You can bed down with our livestock. You'll be warm enough there." In the animals' quarters? Whether this was a cave, a wooden shed, or the first floor of someone's dwelling, as was often the case, this was not the labor and delivery provisions of anyone's dreams. Certainly not a young girl pledged to be married, a teen who'd already suffered much from people's treatment of her. She'd lost their respect and her reputation, and her glittering hope of a normal wedding. She curled up in her separate bed with her arms cradling her swelling stomach, and all the while tried to remember the angel Gabriel's words to her. "Do not be afraid, Mary; you have found favor with God. You will conceive and give birth to a son, and you are to call him Jesus" (Luke 1:30–31).

Now young Mary clung to that promise with every drop of energy she had left and dipped into the reserves of faith she'd been building up all these months. "Don't be afraid. Don't be afraid." The angel didn't say, "*If* you get that far, you'll give birth," or "*If* you have a nice place to stay, you'll give birth," or "*If* your family midwife is with you, you will give birth." No, the angel had said, "You *will* give birth, you *will* call your baby Jesus." This traumatic time would not end in more trauma. The baby who would wear a crown of thorns on this earth would soon crown, there in the animal-scented stall.

Heaven would not be thwarted; God would deliver on the the angel's promises. Mary's baby would be born. Then, finally, in the total miraculous fullness of time, the contractions of birth delivered the child, God in the flesh, from heaven into the contractions of the earth racked by pain and sin.

"There is," wrote the preacher in Ecclesiastes 3:1, "a time for everything, and a season for every activity under the heavens." And there is a time when heaven joins the earth and God speaks into the silence and darkness becomes light. There is a time, "the fullness of time" Paul said in Galatians 4:4 (NASB). On the day we call Christmas, God said all is ready. It is the perfect time to fulfill everything we've been promised. All the promises since the beginning of time.

> The time came.
> Christ entered our time;
> Eternity burst in.
> The time came
> And time stopped.
> Time stood still
> Then time started again.
> The One who lived outside of time
> Broke into our time,
> Into our broken world
> Just in time,
> To save us from our sin,
> To save us from ourselves,
> Through us to save the world.

REFLECTION

Heaven will not be thwarted when it comes to God's timing in our lives. Where have you been waiting, with no answers? What promises, since the beginning of time, bring comfort to you now, in your own waiting period?

BENEDICTION

Dear one,
My Son
Left the wide-open space of heaven
For you.
But only for a time;
Just time enough
To open the path
Back to heaven.
It all began with one man,
Adam,
And it all is fulfilled and fixed
With one Man,
Jesus.
He entered time
For such a time as this,
Such a time as then,
Such a time as now.

PRAYER

God, it's really time, isn't it? Time to say yes, time to change, time to charge not my credit cards, but charge into the world with this amazing news. You came for me. You come every single day into the dismal lives we all lead and invite us to enter into your fullness of time. Here I am. I'm in. May it be done to me as you have said.

21

A SONG FOR THE SHEPHERDS

Glory to God in the highest heaven, and on earth peace to
those on whom his favor rests.

— LUKE 2:14

Shepherds were among the lowliest of the low in the days
of Christ's birth; they tended close-to-the-ground animals and
lived close to the ground right alongside their wards. Even
today, in the Middle East, shepherds have a stinky, grungy
reputation because of their long spells in the fields with the
flocks. But a good shepherd would give his life for his sheep,
would risk wild wolves to keep his wooly charges safe. He
would never leave the sheep alone in the field, ever, for any
reason. They were his livelihood, whether he managed the
flock for others or owned them himself (which was unlikely,
since shepherds were typically poor).

So one night, before the weather got so cold the sheep
could only graze during the daylight sun, the shepherds
tended their sheep, placid and quiet in the hills, with only the
sound of sheep nuzzling and snuffling as they rested. Then
into the middle of the calm darkness, a band of angels erupted
onto the night sky. They joined together in a heavenly chorus,
their light splitting the night, their song splitting the silence.

"Glory to God in the highest heaven, and on earth peace to those on whom his favor rests."

Peace, did you say? Peace in a country ruled by a manic king? Peace in a people who had known only separation from the Holy One because of all the manifestations of disobedience in their tribe? Peace, did you say?

How the shepherds must have drunk deeply of that word. It's used in the same way as *shalom* in Hebrew: peace, harmony, tranquility; safety, welfare, health; lack of strife, reconciliation in relationships.[1] After God's people endured centuries of separation from him, the angels truly proclaimed peace? Shepherds lived in rather constant danger, likely suffering health issues from exposure to the elements year after year. The angels' song of peace must have answered a cry deep in their hearts as those notes spilled out like star showers in the night sky.

And favor? Who on earth truly deserves favor? As poor people tending other people's flocks on land that belonged to someone else, the shepherds could hardly grasp the concept of favor, especially since they lived like nomads, transients treading the sod. How foreign, how appealing, this imagery — that goodwill, good purpose, pleasure would land and rest upon them. Thankfully, God's favor is no respecter of social or economic status.

As the heavenly harmonies faded, the shepherds shook themselves from their midnight vision, blinked widely, then stared at one another for confirmation. "Did we just see this? Did this really just happen?" But not for long. Without a backward glance at their sheep, didn't they whisper in the deep, quiet holiness of the night, "Let's go to Bethlehem and see this thing that has happened, which the Lord has told us about" (Luke 2:15)? There is no mention of a new shift of shepherds coming in to take over for the ones who ran off the field to worship the just-born King.

In our busy brains and our busy days and nights, how hard it is to leave our work and our worrisome lifestyles, throw caution to the wind and our sheep (jobs) to the wolves, and go to find the Christ child? How I long to answer the angels' song like those shepherds, the melodic message tugging on my heart, and me tugging on my neighbors' sleeves, and all of us hobbling off together on our work-weary bones to find this peace child. To experience the community of people on whom God's favor rests. To know that favor, that goodwill and acceptance, that blessing.

But wait. Isn't that Advent? Christ comes, and his very coming demonstrates that God's favor rests on us, and that peace, peace, peace is available to us all. *Shalom.* Everything we need to live whole lives, to live wholly, to live holy.

Peace. Favor. Advent. Christ comes, and off we go.

REFLECTION

Where do you experience internal turmoil from the lack of peace? How about your hope for peace? When do you sense it? And finally, what about favor: your sense of it or the lack of it. How do you respond to the longing? To the news from the angels, that God's favor rests on you?

BENEDICTION

Dear one,
The angels' song
Is the same today
As in the field
That long-ago dark night.
I still bring peace,
And favor rests upon
All with whom I am pleased.
And you, you!
With you I am pleased.
Believe that, please,
And be willing to punch out
From your day job
And your night shift
And come to me.
Because I came in Christ,
Through Christ,
Peace, peace and favor,
For you,
For the world.
Come, now.
Sing with me . . .

PRAYER

Dear God, how I would love to have a beautiful chorus well up within me of praise that comes from the peace you've promised, the peace you've sent in Christ. Help me to know your peace, to feel your favor resting over me, to trust you.

NOTE

1. Edward W. Goodrick and John R. Kohlenberger III, *The Strongest NIV Exhaustive Concordance*, s.v. "shalom" (Grand Rapids, MI: Zondervan, 1999).

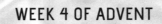

WEEK 4 OF ADVENT

22

THE ANGELS' REPRISE

The Fourth Sunday of Advent

The angel said to [the shepherds], "Do not be afraid."

—LUKE 2:10

It was a busy season around the Promised Land as a flurry of angels made the rounds, from a priest to a teenager, from her fiancé to shepherds camping in the country. The angels interrupted each of these lives as these everyday people tended to their normal duties night after night. None of them expected this breaking-in of God, this piercing of their daily chores with light shimmering from the angels' presence.

The shepherds' reaction sums up the entire intersection between heaven and earth: "An angel of the Lord appeared to them, and the glory of the Lord shone around them, and they were terrified" (Luke 2:9). Terrified. This makes sense to me.

When he encountered an angel, Zechariah was open-mouthed with fear, his heart pounding in the soft flesh of his throat. All these years and not a glimmer from God, and then an angel shows up out of nowhere? And why wouldn't Mary be frightened half out of her wits? She was so young, with a fresh newness to her faith and future, with a wedding just around the corner and all her lovely teen dreams and hopes.

Joseph likely wasn't more than twenty when their parents hatched the plan and he popped the question, only to later learn the startling truth of her pregnancy. He was already worried when he fell asleep one life-altering night, and the angel speaking into his life surely jarred him. And the shepherds, that band of society's outcasts, were absolutely terrified, Luke tells us.

But a recurrent chorus sings through the advent chronicles. "Do not be afraid, Zechariah. Do not be afraid, Mary. Do not be afraid, Joseph. Do not be afraid, shepherds."

The angel kindly addressed the first issue of fear—and fear seems warranted in the case of a mighty angel appearing in close proximity. Who could blame any of them for their anxiety?

"Do not be afraid," the angel said, and isn't that just what we are? Afraid of our insignificance, afraid that we aren't leaving any sort of trail in the world, that we will live the rest of our lives without the specific calling of God, the specific naming by God? Afraid that we will flounder forever in this world? Afraid of tomorrow, afraid that God won't show up, afraid that we can't provide for those we love, afraid that evil will win?

What a gift that immediately the angels told this cast of principal characters and the troop of shepherds, "Don't be afraid." With those words the angels honored our Advent people. We begin eliminating fear when we recognize and acknowledge it.

Still, if someone showed up at your home and said you'd inherited a surprise fortune, you'd raise your eyebrows. "Are you sure you have the right person? I didn't have any rich relatives," and the visitor would look at the notes, nod, and (hopefully) read your name aloud.

So who would blame Mary if she asked for ID, asked for someone to confirm her address? But then the angel zeroed in. The angel called her, as he called them all, by name. These were not cases of mistaken identity.

The angel addressed the subjects by name, and naming is one way we show our mastery or knowledge of a subject. When we recite something from memory—naming something we know (for example, multiplication tables), we master it. Adam named the animals as an act of authority. But also our names are tightly connected to our identities, so someone knowing us by name, familiarly, immediately sets us at ease. Bursting in on Zechariah, Mary, and Joseph was no blunder—the angel called them by name and generously eased their fear.

Hear those words breezing from the crisp altitudes of heaven, reminiscent of God's words to Israel, a breath of fresh air in the dank cellar of our souls: "Do not fear, for I have redeemed you; I have summoned you by name; you are mine" (Isa. 43:1).

In fact, insert your own name: "Do not fear, [your name]. I have called you by name. You are mine." Then take it one step further: List your fear first and your name second: "Do not fear [subject of your fear], [your name]. I have redeemed you; I have summoned you by name; you are mine."

And then breathe again.

REFLECTION

When do you fear? And what, would you say, is your most common recurring fear? How can you turn to God with that? When have you heard God say, "Do not fear"?

BENEDICTION
Dear one,
Hear those words
Over and over again.
These are the words
To the song that will never end.
Do not fear;
Do not be afraid.
I have called you by name.
You are mine,
And because you are mine,
Because I formed you
And called you,
You need not fear.
Hear me sing this song
Over you in the days
And nights of your fears
And your terrors
And your loss of direction.
Do not fear.
Do
Not
Fear

PRAYER
God, I confess that I do fear; I fear far too often, over things far beyond my control and over things I can control, too. Help me to hear your words, spoken by the angels to the Advent people, to hear your song over me, to know you have called me by name. So I do not fear.

23

THE CONSOLATION PRIZE

He was waiting for the consolation of Israel.

—LUKE 2:25

What a long wait. A lifelong wait for Simeon; waiting just as generations of Jews before him waited. But this man waited with an intensity that carried him through the days and weeks and years. He waited, his hope tinged with certainty, because somewhere along the way as he waited, he heard God promise that he would live to see his hope fulfilled.

So every single day he waited with expectancy. He rose from his pallet and swallowed his breakfast; he stood at the wall and scanned the horizon; he watched. Maybe today? Maybe this evening? And when he bedded down at night, he smiled to himself. "Maybe tomorrow. Yes, maybe tomorrow."

Hope provided the drumbeat of his days and the dreams in his nights. Hope.

What was he waiting for?

Simple. But not so simple. He waited for "the consolation of Israel."

The *consolation* of his people, of his country. *Consolation.* This is the only place in the New Testament the word is used in this form. It is the word *paraklesis*, from which we derive the name for the Holy Spirit, *parakletos*, the Comforter Jesus would send (see John 14:16, 26).

The consolation, the comfort, the encouragement for a people in distress and disappointment. And if those words didn't describe Israel, none would, for the people had been in distress for centuries and had been swallowing their bitter disappointment their entire lives. Distressed because of all the years of captivity, outright slavery, and foreign occupation; because of taxes they couldn't pay because they didn't earn enough to pay them. And disappointment in themselves because they could not keep the law, could not make righteousness happen, try as they might. Disappointment, too, because sometimes they just didn't want to try anymore.

But their disappointment sank into the dry wells of their souls, and it ran deeper than just disappointment with themselves. No, much as they hated to admit it, they were bitterly disappointed with God. Disappointment as sharp as if they'd swallowed a knife. God hadn't acted on their behalf in ages. God had abandoned them, just like before when they were slaves in Egypt. And here they were, centuries later, scraping together a living and half of them starving to death and never knowing when they'd reach the end of their rope or feel the sting of another's rope against their hides.

Oh, and couldn't they use a little consolation right about now? They spent their lives shuffling from day to day. They tried to bury their distress and disappointment, taking comfort wherever they could find it. So they overindulged in wine after meals. *Shrug*. So they worked too many hours or dipped their hands in another's till. *Shrug*. So they found some temporary solace in others' arms. *Shrug*. Who could blame them if they sought out idols, if they philandered a bit with the shrine prostitutes?

Well, God could and God did. And God waited and waited until the right time for the people to be desperate enough for a deliverer.

And a few people waited with God. Like Simeon, devout and righteous Simeon, who kept waiting. He knew that the One who had called him, who had revealed to him that he'd live to see the Lord's Christ, was faithful and would bring it to pass at just the right time. He remembered the psalmist's words: "I wait for the LORD, my whole being waits, and in his word I put my hope. I wait for the Lord more than watchmen wait for the morning" (Ps. 130:5–6). He mouthed the verses, gazing out over the city of Jerusalem. "Israel, put your hope in the LORD, for with the LORD is unfailing love and with him is full redemption" (v. 7).

Soon, the Holy Spirit consoled him. Soon.

Simeon didn't mind waiting, because he knew that when the consolation came—and come it would, because God was faithful—the comfort would be enough to take him straight to heaven. So Simeon waited some more, his heart on his sleeve, always on the lookout, like a watchman on the wall, reminding God to remember, to not forget.

What he couldn't have imagined was that the consolation would be beyond anything he could have dreamed. Yes, it would be worth the wait. One day, he would "burst into songs of joy . . . for the LORD has comforted his people, he has redeemed Jerusalem" (Isa. 52:9). Oh yes. It would be worth the wait.

REFLECTION

Most of us live as though this life were the consolation prize, the "we're so sorry you didn't win, here's something to dull the pain of losing." Everyone else, it seems, is the winner . . . but not us. Where do you carry disappointment? Distress? Who are you disappointed in? How or where do you look for comfort?

BENEDICTION
Dear one,
It's a lifelong wait for heaven,
But your wait
Will not be in vain.
Your comfort draws near,
And you won't be sorry
For your wait.
And about your distress
And disappointment.
Could you bring them to me now?
Let me be your comfort.
Let me be your hope.
Let me be
All the consolation
You need.
This consolation is for you
And for everyone you meet—
The disappointed,
The distressed,
The disconsolate.
I promise it will be worth the wait.

Because heaven
Is coming
To earth
Right now.

PRAYER

Lord, I have waited, but not very patiently. I have waited, but meanwhile dabbled in other things. I worry that you have forgotten, or that I haven't listened very well, so that your comfort really isn't on the way. Help me to experience the comfort you promise, the consolation of your Son. Because I know your work is not done.

24

THE ONE WHO LISTENS

Simeon took him in his arms and praised God.

—LUKE 2:28

They were simple people, Joseph and Mary. Ordinary-walk-of life people, cut from common cloth, despite a royal ancestor or two in their family tree. Until nine months ago, they'd been happy living their ordinary lives. But then angels started appearing. Miracles surrounded them, directing their steps toward an unexpected and unimaginable future. No one expected a *bairn* born in a barn, let alone anticipated everything that baby would experience en route to and through adulthood.

This day, they approached the temple, the one rebuilt and entirely refurbished by the awful King Herod. He would soon chase the child held so tightly in their arms, but this couple didn't know that yet, in all their innocence and simplicity. Today, their only concern was to fulfill a little more of the law concerning the infant Jesus. The temple towered over them in its grandeur as they climbed the steps.

Somehow between them, Joseph and Mary managed to obtain two perfect little birds, and these cooed and rustled their feathers as they crouched in their container, not knowing their end drew near. This day was the rite of purification, required by the law thirty-three days after giving birth to a son. The birds were the best offering this poor couple could bring. But it was enough, and they were happy, cooing over their baby like two turtledoves themselves.

Meanwhile, a man named Simeon waited and waited, fingers drumming, sandals tapping, listening for the word. For years he'd waited, listening for that urging, longing to finally see the consolation of Israel. Longing with all his being to see the country and people he loved brought into comfort in their distress and disappointment. At last he got the word, like a player whose coach smacks him off the bench and out onto the field. "Go on, now. Right now." At the Holy Spirit's urging, this man named "Listens, Obeys" listened, obeyed, and headed straight over to the temple. Timing was everything.

Breathless, he drew close to the poor couple. Was he confused by their poverty, concerned that they carried with them only the two birds for an offering? That they couldn't afford even a lamb? Did it matter to him whether the consolation he sought appeared with banners, trumpets, and full court regalia, or wrapped in a coarse blanket and his parents' strong love?

No. None of the trappings mattered. With joy written in the lines of his face, Simeon beamed like the sun at the young people and reached with long-empty arms for the babe in theirs. When he held that child, his face seemed ready to ignite with the blessing. At long last, his life was complete. God had promised; God had delivered on that promise. The consolation he sought, he held in his arms. All Simeon's waiting summed up right there in the baby.

Looking into the eyes of the Christ child, Simeon praised God and poured out a blessing like anointing oil. Did Simeon know that when he praised God, those praises landed on the child? So great the mystery, God with us, Emmanuel. So great the blessing, this circling, this rebounding of praise swelling and filling and settling, there, that day in the temple.

And the blessing! All those long years of waiting, and now the blessing expanded, filling in all the nooks and crannies and longings. Better than he could have imagined.

"My eyes have seen your salvation," he sobbed, his breath trapped by tears, words scraping and tumbling over the lump in his throat, "which you have prepared in the sight of all nations" (Luke 2:30–31). All nations! Imagine that! Not just Simeon's people, all people! His voice tripped, then continued, "A light for revelation to the Gentiles, and the glory of your people Israel" (v. 32).

He thought that God would take him then and there. How like the God he loved and served, the One he'd waited on and trusted for his whole life. How huge, how generous, how perfect, consistent with all he knew about the Lord. This was God's *world* vision, not just the Jewish vision. Now seen, now embraced in Simeon's arms, a child who would bring light, salvation, and glory to the entire world. He breathed deep, oxygen flowing through his whole soul. He thought he would burst with it all, so great his joy, so deep his contentment.

The consolation of Israel. The joy of all nations.

Now he could depart in peace. He smiled through his tears. But wait. First, he would hold that child just a little while longer. And all he could think was, "This was worth the wait."

REFLECTION

Talk about your wait. What are you waiting for? What are you hoping for? How will you know when you find it? And where might the Christ fit into those hopes?

BENEDICTION

Dear one,
It's worth the wait,
Your wait for the One
Who will bring
Light and salvation
And glory to the world
And to you.
To you, dear one,
To you, my favored one.
Can you let this gift
Into your very soul?
Breathe it in
And then
Breathe it out
In praise,
In peace,
In grace.
Worth the wait.
I promise.

PRAYER

Lord, help me to be one who listens. I want Simeon's clarity of purpose, obedience, and joy. Help me to fix my gaze on you, and let my praises roll out like anointing oil, unhindered, everywhere, spilling out, leaving a trail behind me.

25

THE FACE OF GOD

Coming up to them at that very moment, she gave
thanks to God and spoke about the child.

—LUKE 2:38

She was old, by anyone's measure of age, with dark, wise
eyes and holy wrinkles spreading from her bright, joyful gaze.
For years, she waited, prayed, and watched hoping that one day,
one day during her lifetime, through those doors would come
the One for whom she waited, prayed, and watched.

She had been waiting so long, and sometimes, because she
lived at the temple, maybe people even tried to avoid her. Like
a wraith, she was always there, reminding them that someone
was coming, *Someone* was coming. Her very presence convicted
them of their own wasted lives and the longings they could no
longer afford to hear. Too many years of a disheveled society,
terrible leaders, painful poverty, wars, captivity, and depravity.
The life snuffed out of them, they watched for Anna—"the
prophetess," they called her. They watched for her, and
sometimes, God forgive them, they tried to sidestep her when
they saw her coming their direction. Even though her name
meant grace, better to avoid eye contact or any contact at all.
Because grace could be too convicting.

Anna's father, Phanuel, came from the tribe of Asher—the "happy one" tribe. *Phanuel* meant "face of God." Surely he instilled in his daughter this joyous watchfulness, this attentiveness to God. Surely from him she learned of the coming Messiah, the One whose reign would never end, the One prophesied by Israel's spokespersons for so many centuries. And from him she learned to expect, to anticipate day and night, that this King would come.

Anna's marriage lasted just seven years before her husband's death, and from then on, until she was eighty-four years old, she was God's bride, living day and night at the temple, fasting, praying, and watching for the One.

Such faith, to watch, to wait, to center her life on the one event that would change history and humanity for all time. The one event that would override the curse at creation, the fall of God's most precious creatures. For this one event she gave up the hope of carrying on her family's lineage, gave up remarriage, gave up any life apart from life at the temple. Years later, her story would live on, and when the long-awaited Messiah prayed deep, heartbreaking prayers on the mount called Olivet, did he remember Anna and her remarkable love-offering when he cried out to his disciples, "Could you not watch and pray with me for just one hour?" (see Matt. 26:40). How few are the faithful Annas who live to challenge and convict us of our own shortsightedness, exhaustion, or bored distraction.

Year after year, nothing changed for her: she continued to speak of the One called the Redemption of Israel, to talk about the One who would buy back the entire nation from spiritual slavery and slavish living. The One who would cancel out all of Israel's sins and thus restore their relationship with God. But as the minutes of her life ticked away, all her ancient wisdom focused. Her eyes sharpened with every approaching couple. She watch-dogged the temple, knowing that the child would likely come there.

When Mary and Joseph trudged up the stairs to the temple, carrying their tiny bundled baby, did Anna's soul quicken, like John leaped in his mother's womb at the nearness of the Christ? Did her heart pound as she gazed at this young couple and the infant in their arms, and did all within her shout, "Glory! Behold he comes!"?

Scripture doesn't give that detail. What we do know is this: When she beheld the infant, only a few weeks old and snugged tightly in his bundling, she saw her own father's name fulfilled. She gazed straight into that newborn face and looked right into the face of God.

I imagine she talked about him every day for the rest of her life.

REFLECTION

How would you respond to someone like Anna, who spoke constantly about Christ's coming, who haunted the church daily? What challenges you about her example? And when do you find yourself watching for the face of God? Where do you look? Are you surprised by where you see God's face? Who has been a faithful Anna to you, whether man or woman?

BENEDICTION

Dear one,
Do you know what it means
To have all your hopes
And dreams
And deep soul needs fulfilled
By the One called
The Redemption of Israel?
This is redemption,
Your redemption,
Redeeming all the lost years,
All the tears,
All the miscarriages
Of justice and religion
In my name.
Deliverance, rescue:
This One will make up
For all the guilt
Of the past,
Your past,
The world's past.
Redemption for the world,
Bought back by this baby
Bound up tightly in rags,
To a world tightly bound
In darkness.
What will it look like for you
To live into that redemption,
To live for that redemption,
To be part of that redemption
In this world?

PRAYER

God, this isn't about my own small self, is it? Help me to see the bigger picture, the culmination of a sordid history and a heavenly intent, coming together to bring about the healing of the world's wounds. Help me to be part of that rescue, today, starting now.

26

DISTURBING NEWS

After Jesus was born in Bethlehem in Judea, during the time of
King Herod, Magi from the east came to Jerusalem and asked,
"Where is the one who has been born king of the Jews?"

—Matthew 2:1–2

Who knows how long they traveled, those magi from the east,
or even how many wise men trekked after the star in the sky? We
like to envision them on camels, but we don't know how they
traveled either. But see the perseverance of the wise men? If they
relied on their reasoning, on their superior intellect, wouldn't
it be tempting to out-argue themselves as their journey wore on,
and on, and on? That's a long piece to walk (riding a camel
wouldn't be much better) and plenty of time for their minds, or
at least their sore soles, to win the argument to turn back. "This
isn't realistic. What are we doing after all? We don't need to do
this. This is too big of an adventure. It's not that important. And
who is this king anyway? Probably not a big deal—at least,
kings usually aren't a big deal for long, anyway. Don't make a
desert out of a few grains of sand. Let's go home. Besides, how
on earth do we expect to find a new king who weighs less than
a watermelon? He could be hidden away absolutely anywhere."

They could have talked themselves out of the biggest
adventure of their lives and walked off the set.

Who knows how much the seekers knew about the child's lineage or about his parents—though they knew enough to call him "King of the Jews." And if they were descendants of the wise men of Daniel's time, as some suggest, then it is possible they knew to expect the Expected One. But even so, isn't locating him like trying to find a speck of gold dust in a sandstorm?

Wouldn't it be tempting to ditch the GPS and turn around early? Watch for the announcement on the evening news?

But their intellect didn't win the argument. Their souls won. They followed the signs in the night sky and refused to give up, because their hearts, like ours, were created for worship. However long the journey, however risky (and magnificent magi traveling long distances surely were at risk for ambush and thievery), their determination and focus kept them following the star.

Don't we all long for wisdom beyond our finite abilities, limited reasoning, and rationed resources? Isn't the quest for knowledge the very journey that has caused people to stumble for centuries, and then, when running into the absoluteness of God and their inability to explain or reason him away, to turn the other direction toward God?

For so many, mystery mixes not with the mind. Years after the birth of Christ, a brilliant man named Paul tried to reason away the purpose of Jesus' advent, even putting to death Christ's followers. But when finally blinded by the inscrutable Lord Jesus, Paul ultimately said of the difference between human understanding and God's brilliant plan in the Messiah, "Has not God made foolish the wisdom of the world?" (1 Cor. 1:20).

The magi's march led them first to Jerusalem, to the king's palace. They weren't stopping to ask for directions to the manger. Rather, of course, they expected that the one called King of the Jews would be found cradled like royalty, surrounded by all the regalia due a king.

So the wise men reached the king's quarters and announced they'd come seeking the one born King of the Jews. Matthew writes, mildly, that King Herod "was disturbed" (2:3). And all Jerusalem with him. This paranoid king, Jewish in name only, in spite of all his attempts to win over the Jews (including marrying a Jewish princess), no doubt stirred up a viper's nest in his anxiety about being unseated and upstaged. Historians tell us that he sent out spies among the Jews to collect public opinion data, and news of a new king, someone prophesied long ago by the Jews' own prophets. Well, this had to put him and thus everyone else in a tizzy of a tailspin. The magi knocked on the palace door and set the whole hierarchy on its ear.

Had Herod bothered to study the Hebrew kings' history, he'd have known how badly so many of them botched their reign. They practically could have been related to Herod, they were so evil. Far too many did not follow God's ways; they worshiped every idol they could find. And only one king, Josiah, inherited the kingdom and throne in his childhood, but at age eight was a bit young to wield a scepter with much power (see 2 Kings 22:1). A newborn king represented very little (pun intended) threat.

But no, a panicked Herod disturbed the priests and the entire city of Jerusalem with the unsettling news that his kingdom was being threatened. Like so many kingdoms before his, and so many since. Like ours today—the kingdom of self, the kingdom of our own country, the kingdom of our personal little orbit, the kingdom of our profit-and-loss statements, the kingdom of our retirement fund. When seekers come, asking where to find the new King, let's have an answer ready.

How about, "Right here"? "Right here, enthroned in my life. Let me show you."

Now *that's* a right-sized, King-sized answer.

REFLECTION

How would you define your "kingdom"? And where do you look for wisdom? Where have you looked in the past? How hard is it for you to look in the Scriptures for wisdom and then follow what you read? Where has wisdom disturbed you and your "kingdom" with you?

BENEDICTION

Dear one,
Here I am.
Right here, right now,
Waiting for you
To give up trying
To understand the mysteries,
Trying to explain
Or explain away
The unknown,
And the One who knows
All things.
Waiting for you
To stop walking away
And be willing
To live in the middle

Of the mystery,
In the middle
Of what you can't explain.
My kingdom will never end,
But let it begin
Right now,
Right now
On the lintels of your heart
And the stoop of your soul.
I say, "Knock, knock,"
And you say . . .

PRAYER

There it is, that sucking in of my soul, the sucker punch that says, "You got me." I confess I have set up my own kingdom, and that news of a new King disturbs me, too. But please, God, unseat me from my puny throne and settle me in my true home. I don't understand it all, but like the magi, I choose to be content with the mystery.

27

BETWEEN THE LINES

[Herod] called together all the people's chief
priests and teachers of the law.

—MATTHEW 2:4

The story we don't hear in the bare-bones, simple, stable account of Christ's birth is the story of the keepers of the law summoned by King Herod. The magi's inquiry panicked Herod so deeply that he called in the Jewish people's chief priests and teachers of the law, because if anyone had the scoop, they would.

"Where is the Christ to be born?" he wanted to know. Imagine his eager expression, the feigned excitement, the isn't-this-a-wonderful-development rise of his eyebrows. Anyone who knew Herod would realize there was nothing praiseworthy in his question or sincere in his interest.

Because they'd been protecting the Jewish religion for years, supposedly in anticipation of God's sending a new king, the experts answered immediately. They rattled off words from the prophet Micah: "In Bethlehem of Judea . . . for this is what the prophet has written: 'But you, Bethlehem, in the land of Judah, are by no means least among the rulers of Judah; for out of you will come a ruler who will shepherd my people Israel'" (Matt. 2:6).

In spite of all Herod's machinations behind the scenes, including calling in the magi secretly to get more information and try to rope them into spying for him, nothing could stop the tide of God's work. Nothing could stop the advent of the Messiah. Nothing.

Getting on board, though? Not for these law keepers—these protocol police and piety protectors. After centuries of waiting, after generations of memorizing the Scriptures, when confronted with the possibility that at last—at long, long last—the Awaited One was here, they did what?

Nothing. They gave out the information, shrugged, put their hand on their holiness holster, and headed back to their rules. A ruler who would shepherd? Hmm. How fascinating. But they preferred to be sub-rulers. They didn't alter their plans, they didn't chase after the magi, and they didn't bow their knee to the One they signed up to serve and protect. They stumbled back to their beds and then back to their beats.

The chief priests had grown numb of soul as they flat-footed it around the Holy City, safeguarding the law and protecting their own jobs, or at least their job descriptions. To be sure, they would rise up thirty-some years later, angry and defensive, like they'd overslept and missed an important meeting. That day, long down the road at the Jordan River (see Matt. 3), all the pieces would slide into place for them, and the stone that causes men to stumble would become a rock that made them fall (see 1 Pet. 2:8). How differently might the story have turned out for those lawkeepers, the ones watching for the Messiah as part of their profession, if they had recognized him, welcomed him, and worshiped him that day so long ago when the self-protecting king asked for their wisdom?

The king? He believed and cared passionately, although to a disastrous end and the cost of many innocent lives. Misdirected passion versus passivity.

The priests' passivity, their absolute ignoring of the birth of Christ, breaks my heart. And convicts me. After all these years, with Christmas a wildly commercial season that determines the success of the stock market and the profit margins of retailers, is my response any different?

I sing a couple of Christmas carols, an Advent hymn or two, particularly "O Come, O Come Emmanuel" and "Come Thou Long Expected Jesus," rub sleep from my eyes at the Christmas Eve candlelight service, and go back home to wrap last-minute gifts and get the cranberry bread ready for the morning. Just like the status-quo-keepers.

We rattle off words like the priests and lawyers did, but those words fail to rattle us, rattle our cages, rattle us from our oblivion.

We don't recognize the Christ when he comes into our midst. Then in Bethlehem, in unfamiliar guise, as an infant in a feed trough . . . and today as "the least of these" mentioned in Matthew 25:45—a family displaced in a shelter, a decorated war veteran roaming homeless, a child in foster care, a man behind bars, a widow alone in her home with the heat turned down. Come, Lord Jesus, deliver us from our complacency and into your arms that we might reach into the world. Recognizing you everywhere we go, the least of these. Just like the babe you once were, the least of those likely to reign.

REFLECTION

In what ways are you a rule-keeper? What rattles you about this story in Matthew? How have you shaken out of passivity into well-directed passion?

BENEDICTION

Dear one,
I know this is the way the story had to go,
But woe, woe
To those who heed the
Rule but miss the reign.
Wouldn't you love
To write your own lines
Rather than read someone else's?
To chase after the magi,
To chase down the infant King
Rather than keep your job
And keep your cool
And lose your soul?
It's not too late.
You haven't missed it.
The King has come
And you will find him
Looking at you
From the eyes of everyone you see.
Will you welcome them
And the Christ in them?

PRAYER

Oh, God, open my eyes this season. Help me to seek and find you, to not pass through this season unchanged. To not leave this moment without the eyes to see you in this world. Help me to love as you loved the least of these, and thus love you.

28

OVERJOYED

When they saw the star, they were overjoyed.

—MATTHEW 2:10

After King Herod's secret meeting, the magi shook the dust from their feet and the bewilderment from their brains. Then they headed back outside the palace walls to view the night sky capping the world over which the new king would reign. "What was with *that* guy? He didn't really want to follow us to worship the new king, did he? Otherwise he would have come with us now," they must have said to one another, since they were probably wise enough to spot a fake. But not for long did they wonder, because the star they'd been following for so long beckoned them on.

How surprised were they when they left the crowded streets of Jerusalem and stumbled onto the thin dirt roads and small town-ness of Bethlehem? They jostled their camels and travel paraphernalia, maneuvering around rickety stalls and small-town bustle. How loud and how pungent the sounds and smells of the village. Women cooking over fires, cackling hens and clamoring children, the aroma of grilling foods mixed with travel-grime odors and animals everywhere.

And what about when the star parked itself in the sky, pinned onto the dark velvet garment of night? Did they shake their heads and consult their compass, giving it a healthy shake, and squint back toward Jerusalem? "Where did we get off path?"

No, these wise men knew beyond any doubt that the star led them to this cramped and spare space, because they never shifted their gaze from its leading. The entire journey, they watched and followed, robes dragging a trail through the desert. Through exhaustion and exhilaration they trudged forward, a kink in their necks from constantly craning to see.

So when the star stopped, they didn't ask questions. When the celestial body halted over the place where the King Child lay, they were overjoyed.

Overjoyed.

That is one of my favorite words in the advent narratives. *Overjoyed.* This word jumps even higher than joy, an arc leaping beyond plain everyday joy or happiness. *Over*-joy. What a large word, a huge response, far beyond relief or happiness.

We have so little experience with over-joy, or even middle-of-the-arc joy. Much more of our life is underjoyed, and perhaps our spiritual life proves the least overjoyed, the most underjoyed.

This word bursts into our complacence and our complaints, hurtles over all the ho-humness of the holidays and all the almost-trite-but-true Advent sermons we have ever heard. Overjoyed: at last, at last, the King has come! God burst into time; God kept all the promises in this, the most drastic and dramatic move of all time. Overjoyed, they were.

Overjoyed is an external experience. The magi's search took them outside their own expertise and into an eternal realm. In their humility they recognized the presence of a greatness never before seen but always sought. Their entire life journey culminated in this place where the star stopped and their hearts started.

What if our journey stopped at the place of the star, and started again, jump-started by the astounding newness of hope in our weather-beaten world? A star shining from heaven, light splitting the darkness, resting over the One, the only One.

Instead of parking ourselves at every feed stall along the way, why don't we park at the place of the star? Why don't we just get off our camels or our high horses and itemize all we can leave behind: the Herod within each of us, with his lust for power and prestige and his willingness to take lives to protect himself; the long, dusty journey that has brought us to the place of the star, with the marauders en route and the heat of the day and the cold of the night; the painful, foot-sore issues, both past and present.

God, now with us; forgiveness, now with us; hope, now with us. Eternity enfleshed, eternity on earth, the holy invading the privation of this world. Here, underneath the star, the point and the ending and the beginning of our journey.

Over-joy.

REFLECTION

Who are the Herods in your life? When do you find Herod in yourself? How do you shake off that dust and follow the star to the place where Christ is? Describe a time you experienced over-joy. How do you keep your focus day-to-day, minute-by-minute?

BENEDICTION

Dear one,
Just as the star
Guided the magi,
So my Son,
Christ the Morning Star,
Guides you now.
Will you follow?
Will you leave behind
Your Herod-self
And your travel aches and pains,
Shake off the dust
And follow?
The journey ends
And begins
Right here
With the Star,
The Star who even now says,
"Come, follow me."
When you do
You will shine like stars
In the universe
Stars in the world's
Dark night.
Stars.

PRAYER

God, I see more Herod than magi in myself. Please help me leave that power trip and follow the star, follow Christ the Morning Star. Today. With my thoughts, my actions, my words. Help me to respond like the magi, with over-joy. Translate that joy through me. Help me to shine like a star in the dark. In Christ's name.

29

THE GIFT TO THE MAGI

Bonus Reading: The Fifth Sunday of Advent

Having been warned in a dream . . .
they returned to their country by another route.

—MATTHEW 2:12

Throughout the Scriptures, we see God constantly rerouting lives. Certainly this is true in the advent narratives. Zechariah's great life disappointment turned into a great newness and purpose, and what seemed a detour became an entirely new direction. Elizabeth journeyed from disgraced to grace, developing a spiritual acuity that leaps from Luke's writings. At John's birth, his father, filled with the Holy Spirit, blessed and prophesied over him with the charge to create a path for the One who would come, to make a way in the wilderness. Joseph left his quiet, humble life and logged a lifetime of travel miles as the father and protector of the One who would reign. Mary, a teen mother who would still be so young when the child who changed everything, changed the world with his crucifixion and resurrection. Mary's journey from teen to her son's tomb is a scythe of conviction in our daily steps.

When the wise men got stars in their eyes over this breaking news, they followed the heavenly star to the little village a few miles southwest of Jerusalem. Oh, to have the same reaction as the magi: "They saw the child with his mother Mary, and they bowed down and worshiped him" (Matt. 2:11).

They bowed—this is the attitude of a servant, someone of less rank showing honor and respect to a superior. To bow with integrity requires an internal agreement, acknowledging the other's position. These magi, men of intellect and wisdom, these studied and learned professionals—these men bowed before the Christ child. They knew that all their wisdom meant nothing when in the presence of the One who created the entire world. For what could their powerless words create to equal such magnificence?

Rather than being a stumbling block, their wisdom and intellect allowed them to accept the magnificent mystery of God in human form. They needed no explanation of that mystery.

The One who holds the world together (Col. 1:17) held together by skin. The One who upholds the whole world with his word of power (Heb. 1:3) held up by bones and muscle. Eternity wrapped in humanity. They couldn't explain it. They didn't need to understand it. They needed only to worship, to acknowledge the worth of this child. They bowed in servitude before the One who took the form of a servant (Phil. 2:6–8).

Oh, to bow in the same manner, knowing that all our wisdom ranks at a zero next to the Christ. But more than that, to bow in acknowledgement of our own insufficiency, our inability to rule, reign, or run anything very well. But beyond even that, to bow in emptiness to the One who fills all in all (Eph. 1:23).

But that isn't everything. Then, *then*, the magi opened their luggage and brought forth gifts for this child, gifts suitable for a king. But would a king need anyone's gifts, particularly this King, this King from heaven, this One who owned the whole universe and all its cattle and insects, too? (See Ps. 50:9–11.) Of course this King didn't need their gifts. What was the child, Jesus, going to do with gold, incense, and myrrh? But the wise men needed to give them, because then, in the giving, in the sacrifice, they, too, drew near. In the giving, they reached the whole point of their journey—to give the best they could offer to the One who needed nothing but deserved everything.

Isn't this so today? Jesus could do without any of our gifts—he can make absolutely anything happen without our help. But he still invites us, today, to bring our gifts, our tithes, our offerings (our "drawing nears"). But also our gifts of service, our spiritual gifts, and our gifts of presence, kindness, and compassion. Our gifts of time, our gifts of joy and gladness. Our gifts of heart. These gifts are precious to us, because time is scarce and our tanks are empty most of the time. And these gifts are precious to Jesus because to give of ourselves is to give everything. With doing good and sharing with others, "God is pleased" (Heb. 13:16).

But the story of the magi doesn't end with their bowing in worship and presenting gifts. The Scriptures tell us that, "Having been warned in a dream not to go back to Herod, they returned to their country by another route" (Matt. 2:12).

They listened to that dream. They heard with an intent to obey. Isn't that what we mean when we say to a child, "Listen to me"? They obeyed.

And they went home by a different route.

May our paths be different as we leave this time. For repentance means doing just that, turning in a new direction. Isn't that the soul response for us at Advent? May our routes change, may our hearts change, may our vision change, may our worship change. May the Advent change everything about us. May we bow before this One who is the King of all the universe and the King of our soul, the One who came.

The One who comes.

The One who will come again.

And what do we say to this?

Let the adventure begin.

REFLECTION

What about that trilogy: worship, gifts, change. Which are easy for you? Which difficult? Why? Where have you been like the magi? Where do you want to be like the magi? What will it look like if worship and giving change your route?

BENEDICTION

Dear one,
The greatest gift ever
Given with no strings,
Wrapped in a package
No one expected
And so few accepted.
But the gift goes on
And on
And on
When you say yes to Advent,
Yes to adventure,
Yes to this gift of life

Wrapped in a body
That would die
But then live forever.
And you, too,
When you say yes,
Die and then
Live forever.
And you, too,
Draw others to the Gift.
And your yes
Reroutes your life,
And your gifts
And your worship.
Reroutes you.
Let's go.
The path is rough,
The way steep,
The journey treacherous.
It will bring you back
To life
That never ends,
But begins
Right now
Let's go.
Let's go.
Let's go.

PRAYER

I'm here. I hear. Yes, yes, yes. Let's go. Let's go. Let's go.

A CLOSING WORD

The advent narratives found in Matthew and Luke close on a grim note. An angel ordered the magi to return by a different route and then warned Joseph in a dream. "Get up," he said, "take the child and his mother and escape to Egypt. Stay there until I tell you, for Herod is going to search for the child to kill him" (Matt. 2:13).

Joseph fled with his small, newly formed family. Herod, outraged at being outwitted by the magi, commanded the murder of all the boys in the vicinity of Bethlehem two years old and under.

And this, sadly, is also part of the advent story: that people will not respond favorably to the coming of eternity into their midst, to the conviction of holiness walking their streets, to the comfort and challenge of Emmanuel, God with us.

But God has never been running a popularity contest, checking the polls like Herod did to see how much people believe in, respect, follow, or worship Christ. We live in a world where being liked is important and popularity is awesome, and the opposite is to be avoided at all costs. The rash of Internet bullying and the devastating impact on those tormented by the bullies lets us know the tremendous cost of a lack of favor. And how that preys upon all of us, making it difficult to take a stand for righteousness, for justice, for mercy.

But this isn't the end of the story, not the real advent story, because evil does not have the final word. Christ, ultimately killed on a cross, rose from the dead. That day in a manger, when Christ was born, hope, too, was born. And on the day of Christ's resurrection, death died and now hope lives forever.

But that isn't the end of the story, either.

Because the Christ who came to a world that refused him, still comes daily, every single second of the day, to lead and guide and comfort us through the Holy Spirit. And this Christ will come again, in victory, on that last day.

And so, with all the tinsel and trimmings of the holidays behind us now, the real celebration begins.

Christ came.

Christ comes.

Christ will come again.

And we say to this?

"Come, Lord Jesus." Come today in our pain; come tomorrow in triumphant victory. Abolish death and bring life forevermore.

SUGGESTIONS FOR PERSONAL AND GROUP USE

Small Group Guide

First, lay aside all worry that you won't have enough to talk about during this time together. Trust God; trust the Holy Spirit; and trust that Christ has brought your group together for deep purposes. Don't be afraid of silence; most people are, but silence gives God space to speak and us space to listen. Finally, don't try to fix the problems that arise in people's lives. Just be present with one another, love well, and judge not. Souls, like gardens, grow best with kindness.

Gathering

As you gather, open with prayer.

Light a candle to welcome Christ, the Light of the World.

Consider beginning with an Advent hymn, such as "O Come, O Come Emmanuel."

Group Discussion

Discussion can proceed informally. Whether you have an official leader or someone facilitates from the side, the features in this book lend themselves to the group process. You may want to allocate ten to twenty minutes for this section, if you intend to work through the book's elements during the group time.

Ask one another:

- What spoke to you?
- What did you underline or mark? Why?
- Where do you have questions?
- Where did God stir your heart, move you to tears, or challenge you?
- How do you see the elements of your life this past week aligning with the truth you're finding here?

Application

Each reading contains five sections:

- Scripture
- Narrative
- Reflection
- Benediction
- Prayer

The Scriptures are sometimes a phrase from a larger passage. Try reading either the verse or the passage aloud. Read it slowly and with feeling, rather than robotically.

The narrative looks into the lives of the advent people, found in Matthew 1–2 and Luke 1–2. Here, group members can discuss how God spoke to them through the people and events in the selection. Each reading is designed to help us enter the advent story and interact with God's work, then apply that to our lives today.

Reflection offers questions someone who cares about our continued growth, healing, and developing—who wants to see us bloom on this journey—might ask. Designed to prod, poke, and root out issues and expose them to the sun and Son, these may evoke tenderness or even shying away from answering. Still, they are asked so that we can find our lives in Christ, so we can become who we are created to be.

Remember that we don't have to fix one another's problems, point out another's sin, or control someone's life. If you sense this happening, gently draw the group back to the question and its application. We can't force growth; only God brings the growth. Don't worry about silence, and make every effort to honor each other's pain or tears without embarrassing anyone by your reaction.

Try to keep the conversation moving around the group, so that one person doesn't monopolize the discussion. It is unlikely that you will be able to answer all the questions during a one- or two-hour meeting.

The benediction, which means "saying well," contains words that God might say over us after we've intersected with the Scriptures, one another, and the Holy Spirit. This can be read in unison or by a single voice in the group. Read it slowly, and don't worry about pauses and pacing. Use this time for God to bless, comfort, convict, or guide you, and to seal the spiritual work of the session.

The prayer can be read aloud by the group, or by the leader, but inviting everyone to participate in the reading helps each person truly pray the prayer.

Conclusion

Close in prayer, so that God sandwiches the time together with the Holy Spirit's presence and power, compassion and conviction. For an alternate way to end, divide into pairs and pray for one another, either silently or aloud, then have the leader close the entire group in prayer.

Blow out the candle, singing a stanza from "O Come, O Come Emmanuel."

FOR MORE RESOURCES

For a free downloadable discussion guide that covers all twenty-nine readings in four small-group sessions, visit www.wphresources.com/findingthemessiah.

For more group ideas and resources, please visit www.Jane Rubietta.com. If your group is interested in a video conference call with Jane Rubietta during or toward the end of your study together, please contact her at Jane@JaneRubietta.com.

ABOUT THE AUTHOR

Jane Rubietta has a degree in marketing and management from Indiana University School of Business and attended Trinity Divinity School in Deerfield, Illinois.

Jane's hundreds of articles about soul care and restoration have appeared in many periodicals, including *Today's Christian Woman*, *Virtue*, *Marriage Partnership*, *Just Between Us*, *Conversations Journal*, *Decision*, *Christian Reader*, and *Christianity Today*. She is a regular contributor to *Indeed* and *Significant Living*. Some of her books include: *Finding Life*, *Quiet Places*, *Come Along*, *Come Closer*, *Grace Points*, *Resting Place*, and *How to Keep the Pastor You Love*.

She is a dynamic, dramatic, vulnerable, humorous speaker at conferences, retreats, and pulpits around the world. Jane particularly loves offering respite and soul care to people in leadership as well as local churches. She has worked with Christian leaders and laity in Japan, Mexico, the Philippines, Guatemala, Europe, the US, and Canada.

Jane's husband, Rich, is a pastor, award-winning music producer, and itinerant worship leader. They have three children and make their home surrounded by slightly overwhelming garden opportunities in the Midwest.

For more information about inviting Jane Rubietta to speak at a conference, retreat, or banquet, please contact her at:

Jane@JaneRubietta.com
www.JaneRubietta.com

From Eden to Gethsemane— the Garden Restored

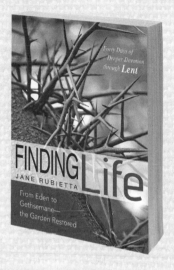

The life lost in Eden is found through Gethsemane. Follow author Jane Rubietta on her daily journey through the season of Lent as she traces the way that God the Son traverses with his people—a path that leads from the exile and death represented by the garden of Eden, to resurrection life like it is meant to be, occasioned by what began in the gospel's garden of Gethsemane. Significantly, Jesus' ministry sometimes took place in garden settings: not only did he come because of what had been lost in Eden, but Jesus met with his disciples in a garden, he prayed in a garden, he was arrested violently in a garden, and he was buried in a garden tomb.

Finding Life
ISBN: 978-0-89827-892-7
eBook: 978-0-89827-893-4

Finding Jesus in Every Season

Follow author Jane Rubietta on her daily journey through each season of the year to gain perspective, refresh your soul, and continue the journey. Tracing the lives of some of the Bible's greatest characters, these are transformational devotionals that encourage great depth. Walk through these stories from the Bible and experience life as these great characters did, gaining fresh faith and hope for your journey along the way.

Finding Your Promise
(spring)
ISBN: 978-0-89827-896-5
eBook: 978-0-89827-897-2

Finding Your Dream
(fall)
ISBN: 978-0-89827-900-9
eBook: 978-0-89827-901-6

Finding Your Name
(summer)
ISBN: 978-0-89827-898-9
eBook: 978-0-89827-899-6

Finding Your Way
(winter)
ISBN: 978-0-89827-894-1
eBook: 978-0-89827-895-8